Responses to *Pushkin: Russian Tragedy*

Russian Authors Society*: It is always interesting to see how one's own people appears in the eyes of the representative of another country. And in this case, moreover, it is a question of: 'Who set the course of Russian destiny'. For the foreign writer Liston Pope our national poet is a symbol of principled opposition, resistance. Although Pope recognizes the name of Pushkin is known to the whole world, yet Pushkin's works (essentially untranslatable) are rather less known . . .

Charles Lambeth: I have read *Pushkin: Russian Tragedy* and I like it. Pushkin is a great poet, and he was a man of honor. His jealousy was that of a man who could not bear the thought of being cuckold.— I also liked *Afterword: Wherefore Tragedy?* very much.

Daniel Berrigan: 'Pushkin' is marvelous . . . and, given the dark times, how cunningly instructive. And the courageous, eloquent afterword: '. . . ever in the hope of a breakthrough, America coming to conscience, a miracle. The people make the only miracles.' Indeed.

---

*Russian Authors Society, in Moscow, is a Government-sponsored writers association. It publishes a bulletin, *Authors and Plays,* semiannually in Russian. This Spring 2008 notice of *Pushkin: Russian Tragedy* is in our translation. An excerpt of the play also appeared: translated into Russian.

PUSHKIN

RUSSIAN TRAGEDY
IN FIVE ACTS

Liston Pope

MANTIS PRESS
New York
2008

Library of Congress Cataloging in Publication Data:
Pope, Liston   1943–
Pushkin: Russian Tragedy in Five Acts
  I. Russian literature, poetry, culture.
    Russian history, tsardom, Petersburg society.
    Duelling, intrigue.
  II. Play construction. Tragic genre, social-historic
    determinants. Classic tragedy; ages of tragedy,
    cultural epochs; tragedy today. Catharsis vs. corporate culture.
  I. Title   II. Title

Library of Congress Control Number: 2007932541

ISBN: 978-0-9638900-7-8

Distributed to the trade by Mantis Press,
P.O. Box 237132, New York, N.Y. 10023

Second Edition, 2010

CONTENTS

To the Russian People

PUSHKIN

οὕνεκά οἱ καλὴ θυγάτηρ,
ἀτὰρ οὐκ ἐχέθυμος
Odyssey, VIII, 320

CHARACTERS IN THE PLAY

Pushkin, Alexander Sergeyevich
Pushkin, Natalya Nikolaevna (Goncharova), his wife
Alexandra, her sister
Ekaterina, her sister

Baron Heeckeren
George D'Anthès, Heeckeren's adopted son

Zhukovsky, poet
Countess Nesselrode
Count Nesselrode
Prince Dolgorukov
Count Vyelgorsky
Count Uvarov
Princess Byeloselskaya
Prince Urusov
Alexandra Rosset (Smirnova)
Countess Dolly Fikelmon
Prince Odoevsky
A. I. Turgenev
Prince Gagarin
Bulgarin, critic
Princess Golitsyn
Madame Karamzin
Prince Vyazemsky
Count Sollogub
Count Benkendorf, Police Chief
Grand Duke Mikhail
Count Stroganov
Nikita Kozlov, Pushkin's valet
Prince Trubetskoy
Konstantin Danzas
Chaadaev
Dr. Dahl
Dr. Arendt
Masha, Sasha, Natasha, Pushkin's children
Idaliya Poletika

Two Maids of Honor, Young Officer, Petersburg Youth, Aide de Camp,
Voices at Grand Ball
Voices outside Pushkin's apartment

1

Old Man, Student, Coachman, Woman in Head Scarf, Soldier with War Medal, Merchant, Servant Girl, Child, 2nd and 3rd Soldiers, Two Workers, Old Woman, Peasant, Boy, Child, Crowd Voices; Six Witnesses

The Scene: Saint Petersburg, Russia, 1836-'7

CHALLENGE

PUSHKIN'S STUDY

With the houselights still down there is piano music playing softly from a neighboring apartment. Mozart. As the scene begins it fades.

In the backgound, as the lights rise, we hear a chatter of young women, a first lively burst of laughter. Now and again there is laughter from Pushkin's wife Natalya and her two sisters dressing for a ball in the other room.

The curtain rises on the well-lit study of an intellectual. Bookshelves, writing table, two armchairs with lamp and end table; a divan in deep red velvet. PUSHKIN sits at his desk piled with books, papers, work in progress. On the wall is a stunning full-length portrait of Natalya.

The poet's features, of a métis-African cast, are wry, grim right now, expressive. He has longish curly hair, thick side-whiskers, no mustache but a trimming of beard.

There are letters spread before him. He touches one; picks it up in two fingers like an unclean thing; shakes it a little. Then sighs: drops it with contempt.

He stands; casts a glance of boyish exasperation at the portrait of his wife—even as we hear laughter again.

Soft knock at the door.
Pushkin. Yes. Come in.
The poet's old valet, NIKITA KOZLOV, peeps his head in.
Nikita. Sir, Mr. Zhukovsky is here to see you.

3

Pushkin. Show him in.

ZHUKOVSKY *enters, excited.*

Zhukovsky. I just got word of your challenge. Man, what's got into you? You need to play this down. Keep it a secret! Hands off people's honor.

Pushkin. Honor! *(Bursts into laughter)* Honor! Ha ha ha! Here is honor! This filth! *(Shakes one of the letters at him.)* My 'honor' is the talk of the town.

Zhukovsky. You are Pushkin. If you feared anonymous letters you should've put your candle under a bushel.

Pushkin. Yes, yes. This slander is all over Saint Petersburg, but the victim must keep quiet. Not a hothead, but discretion's self. That's what you would do, Zhukovsky.

Zhukovsky. I wouldn't talk about it with uninvolved parties. I wouldn't send a letter of challenge based on wild assumptions. Watch out, sir, that's hubris. The great man has a flaw. It is atē: blind impulse leads to ruin.

Pushkin. Look, Zhukovsky, you're my friend. I don't have a better one. More than once you've interceded for me with the Tsar. But you're a bit too cautious, too accomodating. Your fine poetry would be great if you had more of the devil in you . . . So: no, no. My honor wants openness right now, not secrecy. A settling of accounts, not a rotten compromise. I know who wrote this letter. Heeckeren wrote—

Zhukovsky. Do you? You think you do, and take it too much to heart.

Pushkin. No. If someone spits on my suit, it's my valet's job to wipe it off. But this *(shakes the letter)* . . . this is to discredit me. Oh, I don't care what Countess So-and-So may think. But the Russian people will know my wife is not only beautiful, she's an angel.

A burst of women's laughter is heard in the background. It seems to surprise the two men, who give pause, with a look at the door ajar.

Zhukovsky (sighs). Baron Heeckeren had no reason to write the letter. Yet you challenge him, in the person of his son, to a duel.

Pushkin. He wrote it. *(Holds up letter.)* And sent it to seven or eight people that I know of: Prince Vyazemsky, Count Vyelgorsky, Count Sollogub . . . Madame Khitrovo . . . Listen to it! *(Reads.)* 'The Grand-Cross Commanders and Chevaliers of the Most Serene Order of Cuckolds . . . convened in plenary session under the presidency of the venerable Grand Master of the Order, His Excellency D. L. Naryshkine . . . have unanimously chosen Mr. Alexander Pushkin coadjutor to the Grand Master of the Order of Cuckolds . . . and historiographer of the Order. Signed: Count I. Borkh, Secretary in Perpetuity.'

Pause. Women chatter in the background.

Zhukovsky. Ah, Naryshkine.

Pushkin. Whose wife was Tsar Alexander's concubine. The intriguer who wrote this is saying Tsar Nicholas has had my wife.

Zhukovsky. But why Heeckeren? Why the Dutch Ambassador to the Russian court?

Pushkin. His adoptive son, the Frenchman D'Anthès, has been dangling after my wife. Has he not?

Zhukovsky (softly). Yes.

Pushkin. He's been annoying, disgusting my wife for two years now. Well, she holds the fop beneath contempt. But Heeckeren's afraid his son's behavior could have consequences.

Zhikovsky. I still don't see . . .

Pushkin. Then listen. You know the story: how those two met on the road. And Petersburg society knows, or suspects, Baron Heeckeren is in love with this handsome young man he adopted, this D'Anthès.

Zhukovsky. All the more reason not to write provocative letters.

Pushkin. Listen! Heeckeren knows I'm sick of it. What's more he knows I've had duels, I have no fear. So the fop's flirting could get them both in trouble. Heeckeren's afraid. And what does he do? Acts like the intriguing diplomat he is! Only a foreign ambassador would think himself safe to do such a thing. Our own nobles never. He wrote this letter trying to deflect my suspicions onto the Tsar. He is saying it's Nicholas, not poor D'Anthès, enjoying my wife's favors. And then, Zhukovsky, yes, it could put me on the road to ruin: if I said rash words in public about our Emperor.

Zhukovsky. There are those who won't mind if you do. Nesselrodes—

Pushkin (nods). I have enemies. I've made them with my pen: the Nesselrodes, who are powerful; Police Chief Benkendorf . . . But with Tsar Nicholas it's a little different. Oh, I've watched him flirting with my wife like the others. She's the most beauti-

ful one. So he comes here in the morning: on his horse beneath
her window. In the evening at the ball he asks her why she
keeps her blinds lowered . . . *(Pause.)* I know she is pure.
Zhukovsky (thoughtful). Our Tsar is gallant.

*There's a pause. Zhukovsky stares at Pushkin who looks frowning at
the anonymous letter.*
   *Laughter; a rustle of evening gowns. On the nearby piano we hear a
polonaise: light dance music of the day.*
   NATALYA *(passes by in the hallway).*

> Get me ready! Pin me up! For the ball!
> Tonight I'll triumph: du dernier chic!
> Nobility, ministers of state, gapers,
> The entire corps diplomatique
> Watch Russia's greatest beauty at her capers,
> And Tsar Nicholas outstares them all!

She laughs.
Pushkin. I won't go the way of Naryshkine. Young women
from our oldest families, hardly out of girlhood, are chosen to
adorn the court. It's a hotbed of seduction, intriguing. And they
get a warm welcome if not from Nicholas himself then a male of
the royal family. To be a Maid of Honor is a dubious honor.
Zhukovsky. A few husbands have felt honored.
Pushkin. I won't.
Zhukovsky. Laugh it off, like Molière, in the gay palace life of
Louis Quatorze.
Pushkin. Molière the cuckold wasn't so gay. And our court is
not gay. It is wintry, severe beneath the trivial glitter. It is sinister, I think: filled with fear and suspicion since the Decembrist
uprising which tried to end it. And then the leaders were hung,
the poet Ryelev, four others. And a hundred sent to Siberia, and
hard labor: the best of us. As for me, they let me live. I was in exile at the time. But I'm hounded by them. I'm watched, under
Benkendorf's police surveillance.
Zhukovsky. Do you know that?
Pushkin. I know that, Zhukovsky, and more. Molière was only
envied and despised for his talent: made into a court jester.
(Wrily.) But I am honored by the Tsar and appointed Gentleman

of the Chamber so my wife can go to the Palace balls, and he can dance with her.

Zhukovsky. He likes to dance.

Pushkin. Pushkin a page boy! Like a spoiled Petersburg youth though I'm in my thirties. I have ten people dependent on me financially—so deep in debt I'm trying to sell my estate at Boldino. My cheeks are not rosy and pampered. No; African blood runs in them: the blood of a man whose dignity is not thrilled by imperial favors.

Zhukovsky. Be patient. Gracious. You'll win in the end.

Pause.

Pushkin (darting glances). Patient? Win? I'm in their net! . . . I know that devil Heeckeren wrote this letter—but who put him up to it? Who is using him?

Zhukovsky (shakes his head). I repeat: with what intent? What motive?

Pushkin. Look at the elegant stationery. The writing stylized as a disguise: it's a lackey's coarse hand, but the satire's in diplomatic style.

Zhukovsky. Heeckeren would try to quiet the rumors, not stir them up.

Pushkin. Would he? . . . I showed it to Natasha. I said: See this? Little wife, your flirting has brought us an anonymous letter.

Zhukovsky. What'd she say?

Pushkin. She went pale and said the dancing with D'Anthès was all in fun and she had a right to enjoy herself. But she also told me of Heeckeren's strange words, and behavior: the Baron's advances to her, even propositions, upsetting her. Like an old pander he woos Natalya on D'Anthès' behalf.

Zhukovsky. He'll do anything for him.

Pushkin. True, it isn't for himself. Look how charming he is. And I see it too in the dashing D'Anthès, Officer of the Guards: those two and others of Countess Nesselrode's circle are like a magnet for the gilded youth of Petersburg.

Zhukovsky. All the more reason, Pushkin. I just can't see that man writing a pasquinade and sending it all over town.

Pushkin. He's jealous! A corrupt, intriguing man in middle age—he woos the most beautiful creature of the season's balls as a pander for his adopted son. But Heeckeren's not happy and tries to separate them: with a dangerous letter and threat of scandal.

Zhukovsky. Melodrama.

Pushkin. Is it? Last night I went to a birthday party at Yakovlev's. I showed him the letter. As you know he's imperial press director. He could tell the paper's foreign and must come from an embassy. Import duty makes such paper costly.

Zhukovsky (wavers). Well, you may be right. But if you make an issue of it, then what? Implicate the Tsar?

Pushkin. Precisely. Now you understand. They slander and discredit me. Put horns on my brow. But I must be a good boy.

Zhukovsky. Forget them. Keep on working. From that brow are coming Russia's greatest works of literature.

Pushkin. It's hard to work when they're driving me mad. Sick a fop on my wife. Destroy my peace of mind. I know Heeckeren has asked her to elope with D'Anthès and go abroad. Fairly begged her to give herself . . . her body . . . But I must be patient, be gracious, while they torture me. I'm paid 5,000 rubles a year as Gentleman of the Chamber in exchange for my honor. Not much by comparison with the 40 thousand assignation rubles Naryshkine got annually for his wife's so-called 'supernatural . . . inconceivable' charms.

Zhukovsky (quietly). You're too free. You've made enemies. Heeckeren and D'Anthès may be the least of your worries. Half of Petersburg high society, with Nesselrodes in the lead, detest Pushkin. The people love you. But Tsar Nicholas and his autocratic state will never forget your friendship for the Decembrist revolutionaries.

Pushkin (laughs). I told Nicky I'd have stood alongside them if I was here on December 14th, 1825. But I was in exile.

Zhukovsky. See? You're too free. And then you wonder why.

Pushkin (shrugs). They know it anyway. My *Ode to Freedom* was found among the Decembrists' papers. That one, my poem called *The Dagger,* and *The Village* which I wrote against serf-dom—such works throw a scare into our authorities.

Zhukovsky. There you are. You can seem to change; become a conservative; pledge allegiance to them. But stamped on their memories is an *Ode to Freedom* you wrote at age 18, and it makes them shudder.

At these words the poet seems to come out of his mood of gloom. His face lights up as he begins reciting ODE TO FREEDOM.

The poem is preceded by a moment of silence. Like other verse through the play it should have the effect of an aria.
   Pushkin:

> Venus, voluptuous goddess—
> Get out of here: out of my sight!
> But you, O proud singer of justice,
> Menace of kings: it's time to fight!
> Come rip this poet's wreath from me,
> Smash to bits the effeminate lyre;
> Now I'll sing to the world of liberty!
> Vicious tyrants on your thrones, hear hear!

Pushkin laughs. His voice goes low. His slightest movement expresses.

. . . . .

> O children of frivolous fate,
> You despots, now's the time of dread.
> But you, oppressed peoples, on your feet!
> Take courage, stay alert, forge ahead.

. . . . .

> Where ever I look in this hell
> I see whip and chain, and the great maw
> Of exploitation, greed's cartel,
> And the ruinous sham of the law.
> Wild beasts I see seated in power,
> Robed in a thick mist of ignorance.
> They beat the world for a quarter hour
> Until the people cry: Basta! Stop the violence!

. . . . .

> I think all is not well in a nation
> Which sleeps when it should be awake,
> Where vested sectors of the population
> Buy and sell politicians on the take.
> But O, you past rulers, be witness:

When your victims rise up in great swarms,
Then your royal heads fall in the hiss
And roar of historic storms.

Sovereign scoundrel and liar,
O opprobrium of Mankind:
With a savage joy I stoke the fire
That will rid this world of your kind.
On your brow the stamp of damnation
Is read by the people—Now die!
You terror! you shame of creation!
You curse of the earth and the sky!

Zhukovsky (shakes his head). And then you wonder why.
As Zhukovsky goes out, the piano music resumes: someone practicing in a nearby apartment.
Stage lights dim as night falls over Saint Petersburg.
As the music plays softly (Mozart's piano sonata in A minor, K.310, First Movement), Pushkin sits at his desk. He takes up a quill pen and writes something.
The servant Nikita comes in, lights a lamp, then withdraws.

HEECKEREN

EKATERINA, *Pushkin's sister-in-law, enters the study.*
The oldest of the three Goncharov sisters is tall, full-grown, rather strapping. She has black hair, a meridional cast to her features. Far from a beauty, this Maid of Honor to the Tsar's court serves as a foil to the beauty of her sister Natalya, Pushkin's wife.
Ekaterina (happy, excited). We have a visitor! Baron Heeckeren has come to pay us a call.
Pushkin. Has he, Ekaterina? You seem pleased to see him.
Ekaterina (pauses; stares at her brother-in-law). He's a charming and distinguished man.

Pushkin (sour grin). That's good, Koko, excellent. I'm glad my sister-in-law knows the world so well.

Ekaterina (again pauses). Please be nice to Baron Heeckeren.

Pushkin. Why would I be rude?

Ekaterina. You are rude sometimes. You know no law but yourself.

Pushkin. Is there some special reason why you'd like me to be nice to this man? Should I do it for your sake?

Ekaterina. N-no. I'm only asking you to treat him as he deserves.

Pushkin (bows). And so I will. Please show in the charming, the distinguished Baron Heeckeren.

Pushkin, waiting, gestures at the painting of Natalya as if to say: There now, you see?

Ekaterina returns with HEECKEREN.

Ekaterina (seductive). Baron, we're glad to see you! What a pleasure for us. Let your son know he's in my thoughts.

Heeckeren. I'll tell him, dear.

Ekaterina. I think of D'Anthès with respect and affection.

Heeckeren. I know he'll be pleased to hear it. George loves to see you.

Pushkin (stern). Ekaterina, leave us now. It seems we've some sort of business.

Ekaterina (curtseys). I hope we'll be seeing you both soon and often, Baron.

Baron Heeckeren stares at the poet. In the Dutch Ambassador's bearing is an ingratiating note. The man of the world is agitated.

Pushkin half turns to straighten papers on his desk. But he seems to sniff the air. Then he picks up a copy of the anonymous letter, and sniffs it too.

Pushkin (gesturing with the letter). Fine stationery. Scented, as if it needs a bath . . . Baron: to what do I owe this honor?

Heeckeren. I . . . got your letter to my son. He's on duty at present with his regiment. I came to tell you, Mr. Pushkin—we—

Pushkin. You look shaken, Baron. Like a lap dog whose paw is stepped on: it squeals, loses its head at first, then stares up sweetly.

Heeckeren (draws up). My son will duel if he must. He's no coward; he'll defend his honor. But neither he nor I wishes this. We think it absurd.

Pushkin (holds up the letter, shakes it at him). Thank you for sending copies of this cuckold diploma, with my name on it, all over town.

Heeckeren. I had nothing to do with that. Let me see it.

Pushkin (throws it at him). It has your fragrance.

Heeckeren (bends to pick it up; takes a glance; then emotionally). It's awful . . . I'm sorry . . . slander.

Pushkin. You should know since you wrote it.

Heeckeren. With what motive? To risk my son's life? *(He draws a cambric handkerchief to wipe tears. And Pushkin, taken by the outburst, the apparent sincerity, frowns.)* I met him, sir, in an inn along the road from France. He was sick. I helped him through the illness . . . He was 21 then: from an old Alsatian family. Been to St.-Cyr Academy for his nation's military elite. But the July Revolution put an end to his studies in 1830. As a devoted subject of Charles X he came out to fight on the loyalist side. First in the squares of Paris—

Pushkin. Against the people.

Heeckeren. Then in partisan battles in the Vendée.

Pushkin. A common adventurer.

Heeckeren. Loyalist, by family and circumstances. In a France turning liberal he could see no chance for a young man with his gifts and character.

Pushkin. So he came here with his character to flirt, dance, run after another man's wife.

Heeckeren. It is innocent. Please hear me out . . . At first he meant to try Germany. But there he'd begin as a non-commissioned officer though coming from St.-Cyr. The Prussian Prince Wilhelm, son of the King, gave him a letter of introduction to Major-General Adlerberg here in Russia. Let me add what you must know: George D'Anthès is distant kin to the Pushkins: to Count Mussin-Pushkin who married his maternal grandmother. He could fall back on this tie if need be, but the best was his legitimist background. You know the high value Tsar Nicholas puts on this: how in '32 Charles X's envoy met here with your Foreign Minister Count Nesselrode and Police Chief Count Benkendorf; how he came to Nicholas for support and received it.

Pushkin. Yes, I know.

Heeckeren. Here my son's been favored in the highest eche-lons. The Tsar himself presented George to the Cavalry regiment where he's a lieutenant now. This year I legally adopted George D'Anthès to ensure his financial and social position. This is why, Mr. Pushkin, I regard your challenge as a catastrophe: a blot on my diplomatic career, a threat to our high hopes.

Pushkin (lips pressed, thoughtful). Baron, I'm touched by a fa-ther's concern. But if such is the case . . . *(He takes the letter from him.)* . . . then why this?

Heeckeren. I didn't write that. Never! My honor, sir, my rep-utation—

Pushkin (laughs low). Your reputation.

Heeckeren. I'll overlook that, I'll . . . What? Take time, sir, put off your purpose. Think of the risk! Think of my age . . . and the loving heart of a father . . . *(He breaks down; turns, head bowed.)* At least grant us a delay . . . a day . . . a week . . . *(Shakes his head, weeps).*

Pushkin (exasperated). If you wish.

Heeckeren. Give us 48 hours, a week!

Pushkin. Well a week then, a fortnight if you like . . . *(Look-ing away, shakes his head; then half to himself.)* I know your evil wit, your lack of principle. You're a wily intriguer who likes to sow discord—use any means to get what you want. And you don't mind your precious D'Anthès fighting your bat-tles for you . . . since really it's you I should duel, not the vul-gar careerist with his barracks jokes. His behavior is jeopardiz-ing both your careers, besides making you jealous, so you wrote this provocation *(turns, shakes the letter at him)* to insinuate it's the Tsar and not your giddy 'son' who's badgering another man's wife! You're not so old you need a stand-in . . . but that's not your way, face to face. Well, sir, now I'm telling you. Prove you didn't write this filth or else send me your second! Duel!

Pause. Silence.

Heeckeren's brow is knit. For all his tears, emotion, he looks in these instants like a devil in diplomatic dress.

For a moment he eyes Pushkin: seems to gauge his adversary and the situation.

Heeckeren. Please call Ekaterina back in here.

Pushkin. Why?

Heeckeren. I have something to say which concerns you both.

Pushkin goes out.

Heeckeren (paces; we hear his thoughts). The hothead wants to duel—matter of principle. Lord, preserve us from principle. Satan does evil and the end result is good, but the way to hell is paved with 'principle'. I'll play my trump card now, and we'll see if this fortress of principle holds out. I'll use Zhukovsky. I'll use Natalya's kind aunt, Zagryazhskaya. We'll bring him into negotiations . . . my terrain.

Pushkin comes back with Ekaterina who bows to Baron Heeckeren and smiles sweetly.

Pushkin (shrugs, snuffs a yawn). Go on. What is it now?

Heeckeren. Just this. George likes to dance a quadrille with Natalya, but it was never her he was courting.

Pushkin. For two years? And the whole time Petersburg society gossiping, casting glances, sniffing scandal?

Heeckeren. I repeat: it is not Natalya Nikolaevna whom George is in love with. You don't know D'Anthès, but I think you know your Dante, the great Italian. In the Vita Nuova the poet pays court to one lady to screen his deep love for another.

Pushkin. And who would that other be?

Heeckeren. Ekaterina.

Ekaterina (gives a cry; puts hands to temples; tears well in her eyes). But that's . . . this is wonderful! *(She throws her big form toward the fastidious Baron.)* I love him too!

Pushkin (stares one to the other; his eyes grow wide; he bursts into a laugh). What a way to get out of a duel! Ha ha ha! Say no to the woman he loves: slip away from her husband's bullet into the arms of her sister. But that's base! It's contemptible! Ha ha ha!

Heeckeren. You're wrong, sir. My son is ready to make an honorable proposal to Ekaterina. He's loved her from the first, but he's shy. And decent.

Pushkin. Shy! Ha ha. Decent! Why, all Petersburg's aghast at his impudence, and waiting to see what will happen next.

Ekaterina. I accept! It's a miracle! There can be no more talk of a duel!

Pushkin (tasting the sour). Now they'll say he saved my wife's honor while sacrificing his own . . . He's followed her into my friends' literary salons where his fawning and pawing have no place. Both Vyazemsky's wife and Madame Karamzin have warned him to end his tasteless behavior. But the fop persists: more than a Russian would, dogging a married woman in public. And Ekaterina loves such a man? . . . Baron, I know you've tried to arrange meetings between D'Anthès and Natalya. The foreigner sees her as fair game, devouring her with his eyes when he isn't dancing with her, giving her love notes which she shares with me so we can have a laugh together. And now suddenly he's in love with her sister: not a duel but a marriage proposal. *(He laughs.)* Why, you old matchmaker, or pander is more like it—I suspect D'Anthès is caught up in your scheming like the rest of us.

Heeckeren. I'll be patient. The happiness of a number of people is at stake here. My son Baron George Heeckeren is asking for the hand of your sister-in-law in marriage. And so I ask you, Monsieur Pouchkine. Do you intend to stand in their way?

Pushkin. I've told him not to come here. He isn't welcome. *(Exasperated gesture.)* Well, so long as they live elsewhere. And the coward doesn't set foot in my house.

Heeckeren. George loves Ekaterina deeply and desires to marry her. But his proposal is on condition that it will not compromise his honor.

Pushkin. Certainly. The handsome D'Anthès marries a virtual old maid—

Ekaterina. Thank you.

Pushkin. With no dowry, four years older, whom all the world including herself knows he doesn't love. But it mustn't seem that way. Alright then I withdraw my challenge on condition D'Anthès marry Ekaterina. *(Laughs.)* How's that sound?

Heeckeren. Not good.

Pushkin. If he'll consent to those terms, and stay out of my sight, as I think he will since he'll do anything not to fight a duel—then—

Heeckeren. Do not think, and no one must think, that George is asking Ekaterina's hand to avoid fighting a duel. No. Firstly the

marriage proposal must be kept secret for the time being. And
you must not say, as a matter of honor, that the duel is called off
for this reason. My son's honor is sacred to me as it is to him. No
one must say George Heeckeren is a coward, because he is not.
He'll meet you in the field if you insist. But it's not what he
wishes.

Ekaterina (hands clasped; imploring look). Please—

Pushkin (growing furious, his face flushed). Yes because then
scandal. Then it's finished: his meetings with my wife. As her
brother-in-law he gets freer access, family relations. Well forget
it! The house of Pushkin has nothing in common with the house
of D'Anthès.

Heeckeren. Their marriage was in the air before your challenge.

Ekaterina. It was.

Pushkin. To divert attention. Hide the real reason for his flirting.

Heeckeren. No, he had that project.

Ekaterina. He did. He said so.

Pushkin. I see! He was drooling all over my wife in order to
court her sister. *(He laughs coldly.)* I remember the idea was
brought up, but he rejected it. Now you revive it to avoid a duel.

Ekaterina. No.

Heeckeren. A duel will compromise your wife's reputation,
and your children's future. But the marriage of George and Ekaterina will be seen well by Petersburg society, as she comes from
one of the best families. It will save the day. And let me repeat,
on my honor: Sir, you have no cause to feel offended. This marriage will prove it.

Pushkin. Sure. They'll say: look how gallant D'Anthès is—
saves the good name of the one he loves by marrying her sister.

Ekaterina. No, they won't.

Heeckeren. Now I've given my consent to this marriage.
George wants it. Ekaterina here wants it.

Pushkin. No doubt. She's in his power, as D'Anthès is in
yours: so indebted he couldn't say no . . . I seem to see you and I
have one thing in common, Baron: irritation with an overgrown
child. I challenged him to put an end to his pranks. You're using
my challenge to do the same . . .

They bow; Pushkin ironic.

Solemnly Heeckeren exits.
Ekaterina follows.

Pushkin (staring in space, recites).

Great God let me not go mad.
Not that! Tattered beggars aren't so sad—
Not starvation, or a slave.
Oh, I don't set such a high price
On my mind. I might sacrifice
With pleasure what's termed 'reason'—once they've

Said they'll let me be. Running free,
Oh! how friskily I'll flee
Far in the deep dark wood.
Sing in a flaming delirium,
Give up my wits to the fume
Of what weird inchoate mood.

Long time I'd listen to the sea,
Stare with a melancholy glee
High at the vacant sky.
And I'd be free. I wouldn't yield—
Like a windstorm tearing up a field,
Crumpling a forest, as it roars by.

But here's the catch. If you go mad
You'll scare the good people. That's bad.
And they'll lock you up in a cage,
Slap the poor devil in fetters.
Let him rave—entertain his betters
Come to tease the wild beast. Make him rage.

Then at night I will not hear
The vibrant nightingale, so near!
Or the oak grove's lonely rustle—
But only the cries of my comrades,
Curses of uncouth orderlies, tirades,
Shrieks, squeals, clanking chains, tussle.

As the poem ends we begin to hear dissonant sounds and chords of an orchestra tuning up—before the Grand Ball. There are snatches of the same Mozart; also the day's light dance music, waltz, mazurka. There is a theme from Glinka's opera 'A Life for the Tsar'; it repeats, as later during the Ball.

Pushkin (alone). So marriage saves the day like in a comedy. What a fool I'll look in my page boy uniform with that shallow dandy more in my hair than ever, poisoning our family life . . . My heart is simple, and good, but it is sensitive. And they've been practicing on my peace of mind—I can't write, can't begin to pay off my debts . . . *(Discordant orchestra louder as it tunes up.)* Watch, I'll get a letter from the dancing boy asking why I've withdrawn the challenge. *(Eyes flashing hate, lips trembling, he shakes the anonymous letter at the audience.)* You will see! They've made my life a hell, but now I have them in my power. Within a week the world will witness a revenge unique of its kind. Ha ha ha! The fop in epaulets marries a spinstress to avoid duelling a man. Ha ha ha! Ha ha ha!

Pushkin, beside himself, freezes, as the curtain falls.

GRAND BALL

*On the Quay *** in Saint Petersburg the rooms of Prince ***'s pala-
tial residence are lit up in splendor. During the 1836–'7 season there
were balls at Fikelmons, Vorontzovs, Razumovskayas, the Portuguese
Ambassador's, etc., besides those at the royal Anichkov Palace.*

*At tonight's ball, subject of conversation for weeks, turning all
heads, there are some 1800 invitees. At a minute per carriage it would
take ten hours for them to alight in their finery. But they come three
abreast.*

*All this act takes place in the so-called Horn Room leading to and
from the main ballroom. Couples and groups come and go. They linger
exchanging a few words.*

*Through the entry upstage we get a suggestion of dancers sweeping
across the wide dance floor, as stringed instruments play in bursts.
Out there elderly noblewomen in splendid fluffy gowns sit along the
wall staring dully. Noblemen, dignitaries and officials with their rib-
bons and decorations play Boston at card tables as young beauties
whirl about them. A hussar finger-curls his whiskers. A fashionable
writer tries to be witty. But in this room adjacent to the main gala
space we have only a hint of all that.*

*The Horn Room has its share of dazzling period décor. There is an
equestrian portrait of Tsar Nicholas. There are hunting trophies: the
furry snouts and horned brows of various impressive wild beasts
mounted above the mantel.*

Bright lights, flowers—in profusion.

*Princesses, countesses, Maids of Honor in ermine and satin—per-
fumed, powdered, curled; all aglitter with diamonds, pearls, precious
gems in a décolletage cascade.*

*Princes, counts, barons, diplomats, generals, admirals—many in
uniform, or clad with the last elegance; perfumed, pomaded, with their
cordons and plaques.*

The Horn Room provides a sort of foyer for the main ballroom; it is like a testing ground with mirrors. The entry upstage has a monumental transom with low reliefs of Venus and Bacchus, amors and satyrs, vines and acanthus.

Beyond that fancy door is the grand monde pétersbourgeois. But tonight the ballroom seems like a battlefield divided in two camps: for and against Pushkin.

Here are names of a few in attendance, with an asterisk indicating sympathy for Pushkin:

The Grand Duke Mikhail Pavlovich, brother to the Emperor;

Princes, Princesses: Byeloselskaya, Dolgorukov, Gagarin, Golitsyn, Gorchakov*, Meschersky*, Odoevsky*, Trubetskoy, Vyazemsky*;

Counts, Countesses: Benkendorf, Fikelmon, Nesselrode, Orlov, Razumovsky, Sollogub*, Stroganov, Uvarov, Valuyev*, Vyelgorsky*.

Literary figures, beside Prince Odoevsky author of Russian Nights, *and Prince Vyazemsky an important poet, include the poet Zhukovsky*, A. I. Turgenev* (not the novelist), Pletnyev* who is Pushkin's publisher and close friend, the gifted Alexandra Rosset Smirnova* a friend to Pushkin and Gogol; Madame Karamzin wife of the historian; and the critic and novelist Bulgarin who is a tsarist agent and Pushkin's literary arch-enemy.*

Also a strange figure goes drifting, out of his element it seems, among the ambassadors and generals, ministers of state, brilliant Petersburg youth and Maids of Honor. This is Chaadaev*. He is a significant Russian philosopher declared mad for his historical views.

Music plays: same polonaise as in Act One—now orchestrated, but muted, lending the note of historic distance.

At first the music mingles with voices, whispers, gossip which has an edge. We don't quite understand clearly, but we catch names, snatches: 'Pushkin . . . challenged him . . . Baron Heeckeren . . . He persists . . . She . . . Nicholas . . . invites . . . the Tsar . . . tonight? . . . Count Benkendorf . . . Police Chief . . . together! . . .'

Something dramatic is in the offing, which all on hand are more or less aware of, in this place of courtly pomp, luxurious pleasure, intrigue.

The Grand Ball act is one of vigorous Russian music, heightened energy, a brisk pace.

The curtain rises on the reflected glitter of this Horn Room off the main hall.

Music, stirrings, murmurings. Yes, something quite out of the ordinary, besides the Tsar's arrival shortly, could happen here tonight.

The elegant figures drift into view. They pause on their way to and from the ballroom. They say a few words for us:

TWO MAIDS OF HONOR

1st. Charmée de vous voir! You're more lovely than ever.

2nd. You mean since this morning?

They laugh.

1st. I feel like I'm drowning in a sea of gowns.

2nd. Did you see Princess Trubetskoy's?

1st. Not yet.

2nd. Do you know what she told me? I can't believe it! Now I see how D'Anthès' marriage with Natalya's sister came about. The mismatch of the century!

1st. Tell me. Tell!

They laugh in a flurry.

2nd. Well, Pushkin came home from visiting with his friend Alexandra Rosset, la Smirnova, and found Natalya in tête-à-tête with D'Anthès.

1st. Ooh! And?

2nd. He didn't say hello but just went to his study where he smeared his lips with some soot.

1st. Ooh-hoo! And then?

2nd. Then he went in the drawing room where they were, kissed his wife on the lips, greeted D'Anthès, and went out again saying it was time for dinner.

1st. Go on!

2nd. So D'Anthès kisses Natasha goodbye. And, wouldn't you know, he bumps into Pushkin waiting for him on his way out. There it is: soot on D'Anthès' lips too. Such a coincidence!

They laugh excitedly.

1st. Uh-oh. Then what?

2nd. Then Pushkin had a fit. He made a great scene accusing his wife, using the soot as proof. Natalya caught in the act, clutching any straw to defend herself, cries out at Pushkin gone livid as a cadaver how D'Anthès was only there for her sister Kati. It wasn't the first time he'd caught those two unawares! But now she tells him George D'Anthès just asked for Ekaterina's hand in marriage. And then she sends off a note letting D'Anthès know he's engaged!

1st. Ha ha ha! Now that's what I call true love.

Both. Ha ha ha ha ha!

They turn and go laughing into the ballroom.

COUNT VYELGORSKY*, COUNT UVAROV

Vyelgorsky. Uvarov, it's so lively here tonight. Feels like a demon came to the ball.

Uvarov (lip curled with contempt; he is hideous). There's your demon. *(He points from the entry across the ballroom.)* Look at him, and tell me, Count Vyelgorsky. Does this fellow, this Pushkin belong here? If it wasn't for his Venus of a wife he'd be thrown out by the butler. Or taken out in the courtyard and whipped. They say it was done once, on Count Benkendorf's order.

Vyelgorsky. What hasn't been said about him?

Uvarov. And it's all true! Duels, orgies, debauched his young wife, beat her so she miscarried—

Vyelgorsky. No, Count Uvarov. There I draw the line. He's the gentlest of men with her. Maybe too gentle.

Uvarov (livid). He's a devil. But you haven't felt his spite the way I have.

Vyelgorsky. I'm his friend.

Uvarov. Look at the lying epigrams he writes—about his betters! Mine he called Lucullus and only got in print by saying it was 'an imitation from the Latin . . .'

Vyelgorsky. Try not to take it amiss, Count. You're in good company: his lines have stung all our foibles. After all you've got to admire his courage. Whether it's the Nesselrodes, power elite of the capital, or a Minister of Education like yourself, or the Tsar even: Pushkin comes right out with it.

Uvarov. No, sir. Why should I be his foil? He slanders good people with a lifetime of service to the state. He comes here in civilized society, but he should be locked up in a cage.

Vyelgorsky. He's one of the great geniuses, a peer of Goethe but more inspired because truer to his instincts. Of course he has to be careful, but his style isn't so cramped by a Government post, a Jena University. He risks, Goethe didn't.

Uvarov. Risks? Maybe that's why he's written a *History of Pugachev,* glorifying a bandit, an enemy of Russia. As if such so-called revolutionists could have a history . . .

Vyelgorsky. He's out there, amid the life of the people. Maybe right, maybe wrong, but sincere. Well, he's paying for it. Look at him, Count Uvarov. Look at the tortured grimace.

Uvarov. Jealous, that's all. Of his wife's moment of happiness with D'Anthès.

Vyelgorsky. Jealous? Not exactly. It's more than that. He takes us in, and like Cerberus assigns us to our place with a stroke of the pen.

Uvarov. He does look like the 'dog of Hades'.

Vyelgorsky. You'll admit he doesn't curry favor. Would you want his enemies? Look at Count Nesselrode over there: the Russian Metternich, tall, imposing with his grand manner, his astute gaze despite the thick glasses. And look at the noble air of Countess Nesselrode. You and I know how willful she is, with maybe a cruel streak. What a moral authority she has in the highest spheres, making and breaking reputations. Iron character, haughty disdain; mistrustful, fearsome, virile. And this woman Pushkin chooses for his worst enemy! And she returns his hate, and shows Heeckeren and D'Anthès the devotion she has for her few friends, intimates. You heard, Uvarov, what Grand Duke Mikhail called her: ce bon monsieur de Robespierre. Though dedicated to the principle of absolute monarchy she's critical of our rulers. Witty, shrewd, perceptive, she says little in society. She's the Countess commander, with an exacting fastidiousness that makes her salon hard to enter and harder to stay in. Terrible and dangerous, these Nesselrodes' enmity; yet Pushkin never misses a chance to brand them with an epigram. You know the one about her father, Count Guryev, Finance Minister under Tsar Alexander. Pushkin despises our cosmopolitan oligarchy which the Countess seems to embody—you know how some call her obtuse, wicked gossip, even a bribe taker. Witch! But if so then a witch with energy, ways and means to carry through her daring schemes. And she reigns supreme here in this Petersburg society of ours: this courtly crowd ever ready to creep and crawl before a real force which gives it reason to fear. And she abhors Pushkin. Hates him with good reason, and he her with even better maybe. *(Count Vyelgorsky sighs, laughs a little after his outpouring. Then he gives the 'livid, hideous' Count Uvarov a pat on the back.)* Come on, Uvarov. Let's go mingle and dance a little. See if we can't get some fun out of this life after all.

Music from the ballroom.
The elegant crowd mulls, chats, drifts through the Horn Room foyer.

PRINCESS BYELOSELSKAYA
PRINCE URUSOV, PRINCE DOLGORUKOV

Dolgorukov. What a handsome devil that D'Anthès! Look how he dances with la Pushkina.

Urusov. Calm down, Prince Dolgorukov. If you get into the act wooing D'Anthès, we'll have not one but two scandals on our hands.

Dolgorukov. It's divine. Just look at them, Urusov.

Byeloselskaya. A spectacle. We hoped it'd be smoothed over by the unnatural marriage, D'Anthès as the poet's brother-in-law. But he's hotter on the trail than before.

Urusov. Yes, it's worse now. Everywhere Pushkin goes there's D'Anthès dangling after Natalya. He entreats her to meet him, if it hasn't happened already.

Dolgorukov. Soon a duel. *(Clasps his hands.)* Sublime.

Byeloselskaya. A duel between you, Prince Dolgorukov, and D'Anthès' wife if you keep ogling his tight uniform.

Dolgorukov. God forbid! But you're right, Princess Byeloselskaya. Look at her devouring them with her eyes no less than Pushkin is doing. Can the brilliant officer love his Kati so tall and lanky, flat-chested, a real 'long-Meg'?

Urusov. He's the darling of all those who gather round his adoptive father.

Byeloselskaya. Baron Heeckeren is a fine man, so sensitive, and cultured. He's at home in a museum or concert hall.

Dolgorukov. I know Countess Nesselrode enjoys the Baron's company.

ALEXANDRA ROSSET (SMIRNOVA)*
COUNTESS DOLLY FIKELMON
PRINCE ODOEVSKY*, TURGENEV*

Rosset. He's too free for them. Before it's over they'll humble him.

Odoevsky. If not crucify him.

Rosset. He's called the Byron of Russia, but that's shallow. Pushkin's posing isn't what's important about him. Here: do you know the verses he wrote about poor me, Alexandra Rosset? *(Music, crowd noise muted as she recites):*

In the flashy and sterile agitation
Of the great world and the court,
I maintained my meditation
With a free spirit, a simple heart,
An eager noble truthfulness.
With a laugh, level-headed, healthy,
I dismissed that mob's pretentiousness.
Like a child in my purity
But with a fine malicious wit
I cracked jokes like Holy Writ.

Odoevsky. 'Mob . . .' Ha, that's fine. He means the crowd here tonight, nobles. Non dico a populo, said Catullus.

Fikelmon. But, Prince Odoevsky, just look at him. Look how he's changed! Byron was handsome; but if I was the wife of that hobgoblin standing over there, I wouldn't want to go home with him.

Turgenev. Wouldn't you, Dolly Fikelmon? I heard some wicked gossip say you too, et tu, had your fling with that hobgoblin. One night at Fikelmon Palace, circa 1832 . . . Don Juan romped, while Count Fikelmon snored like Judgment Day in his bedroom a floor below.

Fikelmon. Tst. Turgenev, you're the wicked one. *(They laugh.)* But you know, I think Alexandra here should've married him. Two people with so much in common; but Natalya's a lump when it comes to books. Well, I don't envy that woman: Pushkin spends his day writing and studying, then goes off to find you and his other literary friends. It's too bad.

Rosset (shakes her head). I wasn't the stuff of a Mrs. Pushkin. Maybe he shouldn't have married.

Turgenev. There're so many stories about his sensual nature. From chasing servant girls in the gardens of the Tsar's Lyceum, where I took him to enter school many years ago—to legendary drinking bouts and orgies—to debauching Countess Fikelmon here and other society ladies.

Fikelmon. Young man, that's enough!

Turgenev. Brothels, gambling, grisettes. What he wanted was to go to Paris and study, live freely, develop as man and writer. But Nicholas and Benkendorf wouldn't let him. So the greatest

Romantic poet got married—to the foremost romantic beauty of our day.

Odoevsky. Is Pushkin a Romantic? I think a classical writer. Marble style, never turgid. Pure line, clarity.

Rosset (staring out at the ballroom). What a mismatch: it's a shame. A more understanding woman would have loved him truly.

Turgenev. He wanted the most striking one. The most conscious artist proposes to the most unconscious woman.

Fikelmon. And she accepts. I wonder why.

Odoevsky. No other offers! The beaus stayed away. Look but do not touch: as if they sensed the cold unresponsiveness of the fabulous statue.

Rosset (thoughtful). And now . . . what a mess. What tricks life plays. Now he's so tortured he can't even write in the fall, his best season . . . Do you know his poem 'To the Poet'? I'll recite it for you.

Music, crowd noise muted as she recites:

Poet! Don't overvalue popularity.
Rapturous praise can't last: a boisterous brief
    noise,
Then the Pharisaic rabble's imbecility.
Unyielding principle be your counterpoise.

You are Tsar. Live alone. Go your way and let
    them chatter.
Your free spirit leads you to uncharted tracts,
Realizing masterwork. That's what has to matter.
Spurn rewards. They're in your works, like noble
    acts.

Of those who know—your critique is the
    smartest.
Are you satisfied yet, archi-exacting artist?
Your judgment holds: as if descended from a
    god.

You did your best. Now laugh at cultured
  ignorance
Which spits on the altar where your genius
  burns like incense.
With childish joy the oracle vibrates on its tripod.

They pass along toward the dance floor.

COUNTESS NESSELRODE
IDALIYA POLETIKA

Nesselrode. Idaliya?

Idaliya. Yes, Countess Nesselrode?

Nesselrode. Idaliya, I want you to do us a favor.

Idaliya. Anything. Tell me.

Nesselrode. When the Emperor arrives, and everyone is in the ballroom, I want you to ask Natalya Pushkin to come in here. Will you do that?

Idaliya. Your wish is my command, Countess Nesselrode. But won't the Emperor miss her? He usually chooses her first to dance.

Nesselrode (smiles). Don't worry about that. Just make sure she comes here: you bring her. It's important. You can tell her that: important. But Idaliya, you are not to say I said so.

Idaliya. I understand, Countess.

Nesselrode. Escort her in here. Say it is urgent.

PRINCE GAGARIN, PRINCESS GOLITSYN MADAME KARAMZIN*, BULGARIN

Golitsyn (who is very fat). Bulgarin, your mission is life is to run down Pushkin. That's good. The little gnome deserves a literary critic as shrewd as you for his enemy. He needs a little fear of God in him, if you ask me. But could you take time off from your calling, Mr. Bulgarin, and bring me a raspberry sherbet?

Bulgarin. Certainly, Princess Golitsyn. What wouldn't I do for you? But maybe you should ask Pushkin for a lick of his. Doesn't seem he's enjoying it, over there by the far entry.

Gagarin. Oh no? Why not?

Bulgarin. It is red, Prince Gagarin, but the flavor isn't raspberry.

Golitsyn. I love raspberry.

Gagarin. What is it then?

Bulgarin. Wormwood. Like the reviews of his latest works.

Karamzin. Your reviews, yes.

Bulgarin. His *Pugachev,* and the sorry *Egyptian Nights.* Execrable! Taste like gall.

Karamzin. And *The Bronze Horseman*? And *The Captain's Daughter*? He produces a great poem and can't get it in print due to the censor. Then he does publish an innovative novel, something so new, seminal for us. But who begins to understand it?

Bulgarin. I beg to differ. I—

Golitsyn. My sherbet, Mr. Bulgarin. My raspberry sherbet!

Karamzin. I feel so sorry for him. It makes me sad to look at him. After having three children—she's so fancy-free at these affairs, flirting with her Frenchman. Poor Pushkin looks like he'll have a fit, but he keeps on licking his sherbet. *(She moves away.)*

Bulgarin. Look, Gagarin. *(Bulgarin laughs with venom.)* Look how he scowls. Like a wild beast stuffed in a page boy's uniform. Ha ha ha! Like somebody just played a trick on him.

Gagarin. Rumor has him involved with his other sister-in-law, Alexandra. Isn't there a name for that?

Bulgarin. A few names. And I wouldn't be surprised—after he debauched his young wife, and now neglects her shamefully.

Beat her up one night in a fit of jealous rage, so she lost her fourth child.

Golitsyn. Mr. Bulgarin! How many times do I have to ask you for that raspberry sherbet?!

Bulgarin. Yes, ma'am. Right away. *(He goes off quickly.)*

Gagarin laughs; winks at her.

YOUNG OFFICER, PETERSBURG YOUTH

Officer. Look over there. It's Grand Duke Mikhail, the Tsar's brother.

Youth. Ah! Who's that with him?

Officer. They make quite a spectacle, if you think of it, a whole history. To his left is Prince Trubetskoy, our commander in the Preobrazhensky Regiment. To his right, General Orlov.

Youth. Why history?

Idaliya comes into the Horn Room. She looks around. Goes out again.

Officer. Well, sir, I'll tell you. On December 14th, 1825, the Moscow regiment and other rebel regiments were standing for hours, cold and hungry, in Senate Square by the statue of Peter the Great. It was a revolt of progressive nobles against Tsarism: after Alexander's death when there was confusion as to who would be the new Emperor, Nicholas or Konstantin. So the soldiers came out. And Prince Trubetskoy was supposed to lead them in revolt, but he never showed up. At first Grand Duke Mikhail tried to rally loyal troops against the Decembrists, but these were beaten off. Then Nicholas sent General Orlov's cavalry in against them. And noble blood began to flow. It was a bloody scene: soldiers running along the English Quay, trying to get away from the frozen Neva which gave way under their weight. Many were drowned. That night there were fires outside the Winter Palace, lighting up piles of rebel corpses. Nicholas was Tsar.

Youth. Trubetskoy never showed.

Officer. No. And so he's here tonight, at the Grand Ball.

Youth. Ah.

Officer. And Tsar Nicholas will join us here shortly. But . . . to complete the picture: do you see that little guy over there?

Youth. Which one?

Officer. Looks like some sort of wild thing strapped in a court uniform . . . Bushy hair, eyes like nobody else's. Large sensuous mouth all ready to devour his enemies as soon as he finishes his sherbet.

Youth. You mean the poet.

Officer. He completes our history, like a jester in a play by Shakespeare. Only tonight the jester is the hero. Pushkin's poems were found in manuscript among the revolutionaries' belongings. Not for nothing was he called the Poet of Freedom.

Youth. But I've heard awful things about him.

Officer. All true! *(Laughs.)* Like what?

Youth. Well that he's his sister-in-law's lover. Not the one who married D'Anthès. The other.

Officer. Could be, but never mind. What doesn't get said in this court society driven by envy?

Youth. I heard the story of a gold locket belonging to the sister. The valet found it in the poet's bed.

Officer. Maybe he goes to her for her soul, and to his wife for that body without a soul. Whew! Look at her out there, in D'Anthès' arms: without a care in the world as she flaunts it all before the eyes of Saint Petersburg.

Youth. They've stopped dancing. He's guiding her this way.

NATALYA, D'ANTHÈS

Brief interlude of romantic music, low, in the background.

The couple appears in the entry off the ballroom. They pause there, as if framed. They do not enter.

D'Anthès. In Paris no less than here I have seen beautiful women. No one compares with you, Natasha.

Natalya. Really?

D'Anthès. Will you meet me? There are things I need to tell you, but it can't be done here. Will you?

Natalya. You know that cannot be, D'Anthès.

D'Anthès. You reign at the Grand Ball, resplendent as Venus. In my most rapturous dreams at night I could not conceive of such a noble bearing, incessu patuit dea! . . . Your tall figure, your classical features and small delicate head like a lily on its stem, like Helen of Troy as Faust saw and worshiped her. Helen's . . . shoulders were not more luxuriously developed than yours. Ah! Will you meet me somewhere? Please, Natalya? At Nesselrodes'? Will you?

Natalya. Not so close. Pushkin's watching every move we make. Remember you agreed after your marriage . . . no more relations between our two households. And this is how you keep your word—more daring than ever, George, more attentive?

D'Anthès. Oh! Natasha, you're my divinity. Euterpe goddess of music in the Louvre!

Natalya. Really? . . . No, monsieur. Have pity on my poor sister looking so glum over there. And my husband is glaring.

D'Anthès (laughs low). I feel for him. The more cruel . . . it is . . . the more tender he is toward you.

Natalya. When I'm with you I really do feel like the most beautiful. It's fun.

D'Anthès. What possessed you to come dressed in black satin? Other women show more, but you cover up a lost Atlantis. Meet me, Natalya. Please?

Natalya. No.

D'Anthès. Oh if only I could erase your pained look at moments. You have everything in life but happiness.

Natalya. Make me happy by backing off. Pushkin is passionate and jealous. I don't want a scandal, George.

D'Anthès. I yearn to worship you as you deserve. I'll kiss the corn on your foot which you raised while dancing. Your *cor* is more lovely than my wife's *corps.* Ha ha.

Natalya. That's vulgar.

D'Anthès. All Petersburg is in love with you. The youth adore you.

Natalya. Really?

D'Anthès. Please, my deity, my darling.
Natalya. You and I cannot meet in private.
D'Anthès. But why? Why? If it is innocent . . . ?
Natalya. Isn't it enough that you're with me at every ball? Isn't it enough, mon ami, that all eyes are on us—and those eyes are filled with admiration, and envy?
D'Anthès. So cold, Natasha? So self-contained? You're the kind of woman a man shoots himself for. Nature gave you everything but forgot to put in a heart . . . No, I don't mean that! You are the most gracious, generous, warm-hearted of women—like Werther's Lotte. Everybody says so!
Natalya. Really? . . .

The music picks up.
She draws him back into the ballroom.

COUNT BENKENDORF, AIDE DE CAMP

Benkendorf. Has the Emperor come in?
Aide. Soon, Count Benkendorf. As Aide de Camp then I'll open the ball.
Benkendorf. With whom, la Naryshkina?
Aide. Your Excellency, I believe the Emperor has her reserved.
Benkendorf. With Madame Pushkin then?
Aide. She too is reserved for His Majesty. But I'll do as instructed. It could be Fraülein Nelidova, or Baroness Krudener. Could be la Bytourlina.
Benkendorf. Then listen. Your instructions are to avoid Natalya Pushkin at that time. She has something else to do and will need her freedom. Do you understand?
Aide. Yes, Count. But will the Emperor?
Benkendorf. The Emperor is aware of the situation. And I tell you, as Chief of Police and Third Section, Secret Police, that Natalya is not available.

Aide. Yes, Count Benkendorf.

Benkendorf. Well, let's move on. Here comes Pushkin and I'd rather not speak to him. Just look: what an impudence for a poor poet—like a puppy pissing on my boot. But we'll rub his face in it. He'll learn to appreciate me. Would you believe he said to the Tsar's face he suspected him of making love to his wife?

They go.

COUNT AND COUNTESS NESSELRODE
COUNT SOLLOGUB*,
PRINCESS BYELOSELSKAYA
PRINCE URUSOV, PRINCE DOLGORUKOV
PRINCE ODOEVSKY*, ZHUKOVSKY*

The Horn Room might be likened to an aquarium with exotic fish passing by for our inspection.

During a musical moment this impressive group drifts in and forms up at center stage.

The Nesselrodes dominate: Countess in the center.

Sollogub. That morning I received the anonymous letter . . . delivered by our new postal service. Inside I found an envelope addressed to Pushkin. And that was all. Mystère!

Byeloselskaya. But why to you, Count Sollogub?

Sollogub. I don't know why—unless because I was once nearly stupid enough to fight a duel with Russia's national poet. A mere understanding; but you know, Princess Byeloselskaya, how rash he is, how quickly provoked—as if his manhood were forever being questioned; or worse his genealogy, nobility. But the idea makes me shudder now. Woe to the person who ever injured Pushkin. We know what he means to our people.

Countess Nesselrode (fine smile). To the Russian.

Sollogub. Well you can be sure, Countess Nesselrode, that I would not hurt him for the world. And the more so as since then we've become friends.

Countess Nesselrode. Yes and now the little fellow, our African aristocrat, misses no chance to mention his friendship with Sollogub. What generosity on the part of the truly noble D'Anthès, marrying Ekaterina to shield Natalya from her own husband's slanders.

Byeloselskaya. Countess, please do me one favor. Keep loving me and believing in our friendship. I'd rather fall out with our wise, benevolent Emperor than incur the displeasure of Countess Nesselrode.

Countess Nesselrode. Well, Princess, I can't be bothered to swat such a bug. The impertinence of it, really. They say he won't allow George's name said in his presence—seems the poet has a guilty conscience. And he hates me with a vengeance since the day I staged one of Natalya's triumphs—took her to an evening party without his knowing. What a gown she wore: a gift of her Aunt Zagryazhskaya, Dame d'Honneur to the Empress. Her beauty stunned the Anichkov Palace.

Urusov (gossipy, nodding). They say Pushkin has a crush on the Empress.

Dolgorukov. Urusov, c'est trop grotesque!

Countess Nesselrode (nods). Yes, Prince Dolgorukov, it is. Our Tsarina is protective of Natasha: so proud to see the young beauty impose. But Pushkin flew into one of his heathenish fits, insulted his wife, and me too! The madman stamped his foot and cried: 'Oh! I know she'll never miss a chance to make herself a spectacle! She has to please all her devoted admirers! . . . But I will not have my wife appearing in places where I do not go myself.'

Count Nesselrode. Go on, Sollogub. The cuckold letter, and your visit.

Sollogub. Well, that night . . . On his desk were copies. He said: 'Baron Heeckeren wrote this. Rumor says he's the Dutch King's bastard. And Nicholas sees fit to decorate him. Well, he cuts quite a figure here in the Russian capital, intriguing with his adopted son.'

Zhukovsky. So he said to me as well. But does it make sense?

Countess Nesselrode (haughtily). Zhukovsky, sense indeed—to a mind sick and twisted with envy as Pushkin's. To a mediocrity . . . insanely jealous of his wife's successes.

Zhukovsky. Inexact, Countess. He's a classic.

Countess Nesselrode. Sir, you jest. A passing fancy.

Odoevsky. I too don't see what Heeckeren stands to gain from a scandal. But if he didn't write it, then who did?

Dolgorukov (Rubbing his hands). There'll be a duel.

Odoevsky. Was it a warning perhaps? Drum something into D'Anthès' thick skull? Look at the pretty man and his antics: he monopolizes another's wife while ignoring his own. Seems he married one sister to woo the other better. But he's out of line. And we've had to watch this spectacle for too long.

Countess Nesselrode. In all honesty, Prince Odoevsky, Count Sollogub, Mr. Zhukovsky, *(she nods imposingly at them),* we know you are Pushkin's friends. Prince, you send charming stories to his literary magazine. But you forget his sins: his scathing epigram on such a public servant as Arakcheyev.

Odoevsky. Arakcheyev, servant? You mean scourge.

Dolgorukov (turns toward the dance floor). Look at Pushkin. Nerves shot, over his head in debt, jealous, unable to write. Watch, he'll renew the challenge.

Odoevsky. Russia's Third Estate, functionaries, shopkeepers . . . workers, even peasants: they love Pushkin's freshness, and daring.

Sollogub. He told me he hated duelling. But what was he to do? It's worse being a public man than a public woman! . . . So he said.

Odoevsky. Yes, Sollogub. He belongs to the nation. And so he has to worry what the provinces may think of all this. He'll live and die for honor.

Countess Nesselrode. Honor? He's a vulgar pen-pusher who can't hope to understand or provide for Russia's most beautiful woman. Tries to keep her cooped up at home. Threatens to take her to the country: bury her beauty in a village. Look at Natalya out there with the courtly D'Anthès: what a tall lovely couple. And look at the squat gloomy pirate glaring daggers at them.

Dolgorukov. Vulcan mismarried to Venus.

Odoevsky (looks at the deformed, pigeon-toed, bandylegged Dolgorukov). Dolgorukov, she married Pushkin. She has borne him three children.

Dolgorukov. And nearly died losing a fourth, after he beat her.

Zhukovsky. Gossip, sir. He dotes on her. Most likely she lost her baby by dancing all night at every ball. The truth is he's too permissive: wants her to be the star, though he should take her to a quiet place in the countryside where he could write.

Sollogub. It takes peace of mind to create.

Count Nesselrode. Unless you're a Mozart.

Zhukovsky. He's staggered by debts—not only his own: debts made equipping Natalya for these shows; also his father's, sister Olga's, brother Lev's, who appeals to him incessantly. Over 120 thousand rubles in debts!

Sollogub. His magazine *The Contemporary* isn't selling well.

Odoevsky (smiles). Too serious. No market.

Count Nesselrode. He isn't writing like he used to. Not the leader anymore.

Byeloselskaya. Mr. Zhukovsky, aren't the critics panning his new works? I heard he was a reactionary.

Zhukovsky. He pays other's debts and drowns in his own. Can't find peace and quiet but only worries himself sick. How even to pay the rent: 4300 rubles a year for their new Admiral Street apartment.

Odoevsky. And amid it all comes an anonymous letter: a slanderous lampoon is sent around the city . . . When I visited him at home the other day, he took me in the nursery and showed me his children. With a sad smile he took Sasha, the little boy, in his arms. It seems the demonic genius is a tender father. I asked him why he got married, and he said he didn't want to. He was restless and wanted to go abroad and study, but they wouldn't let him.

Countess Nesselrode. Gentlemen, it's no time to grow sentimental over a poetaster. I'm so tired of his scowls and posturing.

Count Nesselrode. Byron's ape.

Countess Nesselrode. And now he's been rude to our good Baron Heeckeren. Challenged D'Anthès to a duel for no reason. On a supposition. Jealous!

Odoevsky. Countess, with all respect to you, he's a national treasure. And if there's a duel, as I fear there may still be, we could lose him in his thirties.

Zhukovsky. And then content ourselves with the great works he's given us: *Yevgeny Onyegin, Boris Godunov, The Bronze Horseman, The Captain's Daughter,* such a wealth of narrative poems, lyrics, fairy tales, short stories, his short plays like *Mozart and Salieri* tossed off it seems in a spare moment. So many masterpieces, by the batch! But now he hesitates. And his 'middle period', the great Russian realist—will it get started?

Odoevsky. Congratulations to the author of that hate letter.

Sollogub. There was another, a second one. Have you heard?

Dolgorukov (happily). Let's duel.

THE EMPEROR IS COMING!

Suddenly a hush.

Voices. The Emperor! It's the Emperor! Tsar Nicholas is coming! He is here!

Whispers, emotion. The elegant crowd seems to undulate like wheat in a field toward the source of excitement.

Music: stirring bars from Glinka's 'A Life For the Tsar'.

In a rustle of gowns people press forward and jockey to watch Nicholas make his entry.

Voices emerge among the Ministers of State, foreign ambassadors, noblemen and noblewomen; generals and military men in uniform, their chests aglitter with medals, sashes.

Voice 1. Look! He's nodding to la Londondery.

Voice 2. You mean that one?

Voice 3. Wife of an English general.

Voice 1. What emeralds, what . . . diamonds!

Voice 4. A treasure chest.

Voices . . .

In the Horn Room sits PRINCE TRUBETSKOY, *alone for a moment, catching his breath.*

PUSHKIN *also seeking a respite by himself, away from the throng and the Tsar, comes in.*

Pushkin. Prince Trubetskoy, what are you doing here? This place with its horns is not for your likes, an officer in the Horse Cavalry, not yet married. This room is for the married men, all the husbands, our brothers.

Trubetskoy. That'll do, Pushkin. Even in public, at the Grand Ball you ignore the Emperor? Seek any pretext to vent your bile?

Prince Trubetskoy goes out.

Pushkin takes a crumpled piece of paper from his pocket. Reads it at a glimpse—then folds and puts it back.

Pushkin. So they send me a second letter. Another one . . . to provoke me . . . destroy me. It won't end. *(He moves to the entry and, staring out at the ballroom, recites to himself as if thinking):*

I'm not so wild about unbridled ecstasies,
Extravagant embraces, raptures, sensuous frenzies,
Groans, shrieks, pleadings of the youthful bacchant
When, writhing in my arms, she'll moan, strain, pant
In a transport of caresses, tongue darting viperous
    kisses,
Hurrying our climax with her squeals, her lustful
    hisses . . .

As Pushkin recites, PRINCE DOLGORUKOV *enters from the other door; sneaks up behind him; and makes the cuckold sign with index and little finger behind the poet's head. This is for all in the ballroom to see. There is a burst of laughter from the dance floor.*

No, you're much more lovable, meek and humble, little
    wife.
But O what a torture of happiness is our life
Together when, having laughed at my passionate pleas
You give yourself with a shrug to the poor man, on his
    knees,
In your cool sort of pudor, barely accepting,
    responding

To my crazed desire, hardly opening, receiving . . .
Then at last you get stirred up, excited more and more
And sharing my pleasure you shudder, despite
   yourself, at the core.

*Prince Dolgorukov goes out—back into the ballroom: brushing past
his victim who looks at him.*
   *Now Pushkin, shaking his head a little, backs away and moves to
the far wall. There he stands face to face with a hunting trophy—great
furry snout, white teeth, impressive set of antlers.*
   Just then we hear the voice and laughter of GEORGE D'ANTHÈS.
   D'Anthès. Leave me alone for now, Ekaterina. No, *ma légitime,*
I've business to tend to . . . in here. See you in a few minutes.
   *Pushkin half turns. Then, on an impulse, he takes down the stag's
head into his hands, hefts it, and puts it over his own head like a mask.
It fits!*
   *Then Pushkin freezes in place—his legs, torso unseen behind a ma-
hogany table with a lamp on it.*
   *D'Anthès comes in airily; looks around; doesn't notice the presence
of Natalya's husband.*
   *From outside: strains of period music. There is a sense of distance in
time, nostalgia for another era. The music is not loud.*

   Enter IDALIYA POLETIKA, *all but dragging* NATALYA *into
the Horn Room. Natalya gives a gasp; she winces, sighs as D'Anthès
steps forward to meet her.*
   D'Anthès. Natasha, I must see you alone.
   Natalya. You want to see me?
   D'Anthès approaches her, with a nod to Idaliya.
   Idaliya. Please excuse me. There's something I have to do. *(She
goes.)*
   In the entry stands an officer who seems to keep watch.
   D'Anthès. Natalya, I had to be alone with you: where no one
can hear us. I'm in despair. I'm not sure what I'll do if you say no
now: maybe kill myself. Yes, I won't survive such a rejection.
And it would be a death sentence not only for myself, not only
one person who loves you, but for your sister as well. I know
Ekaterina won't want to live after my suicide. So you see two
people could die, Natalya, because of your coldheartedness. Or

no, I don't mean that! I know how loving, how generous, how kind you are to others. But let's say because of . . . your misplaced sense of . . .

D'Anthès, in throes of passion, has lost his dashing air. A hand to his heart, as if in pain, he goes on his knees before her.

Natalya. Ah! You're unfair. Have I led you on?

She half turns. He draws closer.

D'Anthès. Oh you beautiful woman! Beauty has done its work, and now I'm at your feet. I can't help myself any longer. I must either have you tonight, or die.

Natalya. Are you mad? My husband is here—he's—

D'Anthès. Elope with me! We'll run away! Far, far from that swarthy dwarf who never should have dared look at you, let alone make love to such a goddess. You know it's true! You know it is I—we who are destined for one another. I love you, I love you! Please, my darling, let us spend our lives together!

Natalya. But you are married.

D'Anthès. If you don't give yourself to me after all this time— two years, Natalya, two years I've loved and suffered—

Natalya. Married to my sister.

D'Anthès. But you were only toying with love and with my feelings. You're unwilling to do what your heart tells you—and why? For the sake of some . . . *(grits his teeth)* . . . of prudery . . . a childish fear that'll keep you unhappy always. But I . . . I . . .

He pulls out a small revolver.

Natalya. Ah!

D'Anthès. I swear I will blow my brains out if you don't relent and take pity on a man who loves you truly. Come with me now. Come! There is a room—no one will—

Natalya. No! You are—I can't— *(She pulls away; she looks here, there: turns this way and that, like in a cage.)* No—

D'Anthès *(panting)*. Please! Come! Please—

Natalya. You lured me in here. I can't do what you say—even if there weren't people who would miss our presence, starting with my husband.

D'Anthès *(gnashing)*. Jealous mongrel. It doesn't concern him!

Natalya. It does, George, and it cannot be. We've enjoyed one another and can go on doing so if you'll keep your head, and draw back! I won't say I don't care for you, but . . . but this . . . Why did Idaliya bring me in here? You're in league? She hates

Pushkin ever since he snubbed her trying to get closer to him.
No, George, this isn't it. I have to go.

D'Anthès. Please, Natasha! My love, my—my fate!

Natalya. You said you respected my honor. Your wife's sister.
You're not doing that.

D'Anthès (groans). Why do you make me suffer like this? I
must have you—to live! If not I'll *(moans at her feet)*—I could deal
with Russia's enemy on the battlefield, but this enemy *(taps his
heart)* . . . this enemy is too much for me!

Natalya. Get up.

D'Anthès. I'll shoot myself before this night is over!

Natalya. No.

*She turns to rush from the room. She sails out past the officer keep-
ing watch.*

There is a low, malicious laughter.

*D'Anthès gives a little jolt. He looks around—then gets to his feet.
He spends a moment brushing himself off. And then, as the laughter
continues, he turns to go. Handsome blond head high with a thought
for his dignity, he makes to leave the Horn Room.*

But the laughter becomes a voice.

Pushkin (immobile; still in the stag's head). Put the gun away,
you imbecile.

D'Anthès (turns back with a start). What? Who's there?

Pushkin (strange laughter, deep, cavernous). Me.

D'Anthès (glances at the exit to ballroom). Wait, Natalya.

Pushkin. Forget her. Show's over, D'Anthès.

D'Anthès. I beg your pardon. Who is this?

Pushkin (more low laughter; he comes forward, still masked). The
stone guest.

*D'Anthès (breaks into laughter as the boar's head in a Gentleman of
the Chamber's uniform seems to detach itself from the wall and come
forward).* Oui, monsieur?

Pushkin. Stroganov's bastard daughter set this up.

D'Anthès (chuckles calmly, friendly). Idaliya?

Pushkin. But why?

D'Anthès (glances toward the ballroom, turning to go). Maybe she
doesn't like your long fingernails, like a devil's.

Pushkin. Just hold on there. I'm not done.

D'Anthès (impatient now, turns back, surly). Eh bien, what can I do for you?

Pushkin (takes off the stag's head, as D'Anthès laughs despite himself). You could stop being a cowardly fop, if that wasn't your deepest nature.

D'Anthès. Watch your insults. They'll have consequences.

Pushkin. Will they? Good. That's what I want. I've let your disgusting behavior go on long enough—which is why I welcomed the filthy letter sent around Petersburg by your pimp of a 'father'. I knew the time had come to make you play a role so pitiful, that my wife and I, amused by your cowardice, your lying subservience, sir, would have another good laugh at you. For a moment you troubled her, I admit it. But then your 'grand and sublime' passion was beneath contempt—a thing of instinct, loathsome. Tell me: is it comme il faut when the diplomatic representative of a crowned head acts as his so-called son's pimp? when he tells you what sorry role you'll play, what vulgar jokes and remarks you'll make, what empty-headed behavior you'll engage in? But all that comes easily for you. And like an obscene old woman the baron pander tags along after my wife and lisps of his putative son's true love. And when you were sick at home with syphilis he said you were dying of love for her. And then he'd mutter with soul: Give me back my son . . . I could've made a laughingstock of the two of you. I had you in my hands, but I let it go on condition I wouldn't have to lay eyes on your likes anymore, or my wife be bothered by the bawd Heeckeren. Someone like him, and like you, has no business speaking to a decent woman. Do you understand? Am I clear? Your sins are many: abject fawning, vulgar attempts at wit, posing at devotion and a tragic passion, the way you did just now. I'm calling you on them.

D'Anthès. You think you can say such things to me?

Pushkin. I said them.

D'Anthès. I'll send you my second tomorrow. Have him settle with yours on the site and conditions.

Pushkin. I'll be waiting. The bloodier the better. *(He puts his stag's head back on and, clicking his heels, gives the Officer of the Guards a salute.)*

D'Anthès bows and goes out.
Pushkin (recites).

'. . . O heavy, heavy
The stone guest's handshake—
Let go! Let go I say, let me go, ah!
I'm dying. Life is over. Doña Anna!'

After reciting Pushkin gives a laugh: happy now, relieved. The die is cast.

MAD CHAADAEV

Pushkin. Ah. It's Chaadaev, the mystic historian.

CHAADAEV *comes wandering into the Horn Room where Pushkin stands staring from his trophy-head into space.*

The liberal philosopher P. Y. Chaadaev, in the uniform of his early years as Colonel of the Hussars, cuts a striking figure. Tall, slender, still handsome with a high bald forehead, he gazes like myopia trying to focus. The note is disparity: dishevelled wildness bundled in a military uniform.

Chaadaev (bows slightly while looking quizzically at the beast dressed up as a page boy). Are you the soul of Russia?

Pushkin. A soul with horns.

Chaadaev (reaches, touches the tip of a horn). Let's examine that point.

Pushkin. Увы. Ouch, that hurts.

Chaadaev. History has a soul. *(He nods a little, like a child agreeing for you.)*

Pushkin. Has it?

Chaadaev. It went mad the same day I did—mad as the Great Schism, mad as Greek Orthodoxy. That day in 1054 A.D. history lost its way, and I was declared 'officially' crazy. Am I? *(He stoops, and stares fixedly into the eyes of the much shorter . . . stag.)*

Pushkin. No.

Chaadaev. It's a pleasure talking to you . . . I have enemies.

Pushkin. Do you?

Chaadaev. I make them without knowing it.

Pushkin (forgetting he's masked). Chaadaev, I'm glad to see you. Once, when I was young, our friendship took the place of happiness. But we've met less the past few years. They say you've gotten to be a tourist attraction.

Chaadaev. The beast speaks for incommunicado Man.

Pushkin. What a shallow schoolboy I was in those days at Tsarskoye Selo, our Tsar's training school for the nobility.

Chaadaev. And look at you now. Well-trained I must say: a noble beast.

Pushkin. Back then I had no care, no purpose or system. Just couldn't wait to go out in the world and gad about, rack up conquests, have duels. Oh, I was so taken by Chaadaev: the young dandy in uniform with his wit and elegance, cynical courtesy among companions. So many things we spoke of together, Shakespeare, French skepticism, the philosophy of Locke. And then poetry became more than a light neoclassical pastime for me; it grew to be serious and real. You jolted me into consciousness.

Chaadaev (goes to the mantel, takes down another furry animal's head and puts it on). Greetings!

Pushkin. Greetings, brother. You're looking well.

Chaadaev. 'Officially' cured! Now I am duly august! Now I've got my protective covering, and can go among the other august personages, out there! *(Peers out, bending forward. Then straightens; thrusts out his chest, salutes.)*

Pushkin. No longer under 'medical surveillance' for your views?

Chaadaev. Mad! Mad as hell because history is mad! Mad as the Semyenovsky Regiment when I marched to Paris with it in 1812. Mad as one country invading and occupying another. Mad as Russia with its serfdom like a fixation: a few decorated beasts living in luxury while the great herd lives poor and does all the work.

Pushkin. Not so loud. You'll be an august elk, in Siberia.

Chaadaev. The editor of my *Philosophical Letters* was sent to Siberia! That moose Uvarov sent him.

Pushkin. Shh, he's just outside.

Chaadaev. Count Uvarov, Minister of Popular Enlightenment, President of the Academy of Science, Chairman of the Censorship, a moose! Says: lock up mad Chaadaev with his theses of Russia adrift in history without a destiny unless for evil, Russia ignorant of its historic duty, Russia without social justice, Russia without men and women of principle, without truth! . . . Mad Chaadaev! Ha ha ha! Pack him off to Siberia, or America where a moose feels at home. Because Russia has more wars to fight, more wars of Oleg and Svyatoslav; more glorious wars of appanage. Bad adventures, 'sad and grand invasions', as my young friend Pushkin has said.

Pushkin. Has he?

Chaadaev. There's a real madman for you. *(Nods at him.)* And he's mad enough to think the two Ivans, Ryurik, the accession to the throne of these officially sane Romanovs of ours, Boris Godunov and Peter the Great, Catherine the Second and Alexander who led us to Paris—my young friend Pushkin calls this 'the youth of the peoples'. Well I call it the bloody mire of prehistory—before a single cell of principle was engendered; before a first measly mite of conscience in all universal eternity; before a word of truth was spoken by some poor damned madman in this immemorial night of Russia! . . .

Pushkin. Russia.

Chaadaev. Ha ha ha! Lock him up! You see he is an honorary madman. Ha ha ha!

Pushkin. Chaadaev wears a halo of martyrdom and courage in this Russia where it is our curse, men of talent, to have been born.

Chaadaev. Ecce beast! Ah-ha-ha-a-a-aaaa! . . .

In the true style of madmen he goes running out, half-crouching, glancing around—a horned stag into the ballroom where we hear a burst of laughter, cries, sighs.

Pushkin takes off the furry head and follows him solemnly.

COUNT BENKENDORF, PRINCE DOLGORUKOV

Benkendorf. Our plan is working, Dolgorukov.

Dolgorukov. So it seems, Count Benkendorf. What a master that Countess Nesselrode. The second anonymous letter, which we sent yesterday, has Pushkin primed with hate and anger. He was beside himself when he came here tonight. When the apple's ripe, it falls. *(Rubs his hands with a grin.)* And now the challenge.

Benkendorf. Now the duel.

Dolgorukov. He fell right into it. Such a child. They say he's gloomy with his wife but gay and happy away from her. Attentive and tender when they're with certain people; then brusque, even coarse when with others, like Azinkoy, as they call the older sister, Alexandrina.

Benkendorf. We have him by his honor.

Dolgorukov. The bull by the horns. Have you seen him? I can't help laughing at the little man looking frazzled, eyes bloodshot, features twitching. His face looks jaundiced.

Benkendorf. He's said to be a crack shot. Well, D'Anthès is a military man, in practice.

Dolgorukov (chuckles low). The cuckold letter was a tour de force, if I do say so myself.

Benkendorf (low). Don't gloat. And no word, no slightest suspicion, ever, that the Emperor . . .

Dolgorukov. Of course, Count Benkendorf.

Benkendorf. We're using two foreigners to rid ourselves of a pest. For a long time we've hounded him. Now he's at bay. Now the end. We'll have Count Stroganov work on Heeckeren who'll run right to him for advice. No other course: duel.

Dolgorukov. Heeckeren's so in love with D'Anthès he had to pander for him with Natalya.

Benkendorf. Almost as depraved as you are.

Dolgorukov. Ah. Ha!

Benkendorf. A twisted skein. But now Heeckeren's ruined himself here in Russia. No more maneuvering, like the surprise marriage. For the thing is on the march, and we are going to the field of honor. Now Pushkin, the renegade to his class, the traitor, will perish. His name and his poetry will be forgotten. We'll see to it. For this is in the best interest of Russia and our beloved Tsar.

Dolgorukov. So be it, Count Benkendorf.

Benkendorf. So be it.

Dolgorukov (softly). Amen.

CURTAIN

DUEL

DRAWING ROOM AT THE PUSHKINS

Pushkin's sister-in-law, ALEXANDRA, *comes in.*
Alexandra. What are you doing?
Pushkin. Oh, Alexandra, just a few last *(he writes)* . . . just details to do with my magazine. Something about a translation.
Alexandra. Lieutenant Colonel Danzas is here to see you.
Pushkin. Danzas? Good, show him in. Thanks, dear.

Enter DANZAS.
Pushkin (rises with a smile, energetically, hand held out). Constantine Danzas, I'm so glad I found you! I was at Razumovskys and asked a British official to be my second, but he said no when I wouldn't tell him the ins and outs. There won't be any more negotiations.
Danzas (stares at him). Long time, Pushkin.
Pushkin (laughs happily). We haven't seen each other much since old school days at the Lyceum. Ha ha! Witty Danzas, fun-loving, life-loving but not too much! You know the ancient Greeks had a good word, philozoos: by this they meant over-fond of life, cowardly. I heard you were wounded in the Turkish War in '28. Ha! In school you were typographer of our magazine, The Lyceum Sage, remember? Danzas the loyal friend, brave and honest, carefree.
Danzas. Today I'm not carefree. The world knows you're right. Why risk yourself?

Pushkin. I know what I have to do. That October day when
we met for the 25th Anniversary of our class I wasn't feeling
as good as today. No boisterous poem for the occasion: I stood
up and read in the tone of an elegy for classmates no longer
with us. The empty chairs made us sad; and when I recited, I
broke down, tears in my eyes, and couldn't go on . . . Remember? But today I'd do better. Hold on. *(He gives a chuckle and
recites.)*

> The more times our Lycée
> Comes together in reunion,
> The more a tentativeness may
> Hinder sacred communion.
> Sparser we are. Happiness blends
> With sadness on the special day,
> Remembering departed friends.
> We sing a less exultant way.
>
> Thus storms sweeping over the earth
> Blew an unexpected breath
> On us—old classmates at our mirth
> Stunned by a mood of death.
> We came of age. Fate designated
> Even us for the trials of men.
> We drank, we sang, commemorated;
> The spirit of death went among us then.
>
> Six settings without occupants,
> Six friends we won't see anymore:
> They rest among the elements—
> Here and there, in the field, at war,
> Cozy home or far distant place.
> They sickened, they suffered, then slept:
> Candle in dank gloom of space.
> And over each of them we wept.
>
> And it seems, up ahead in the line,
> I hear my Delvig calling me,
> Comrade of dreams, springtime and wine,

Exuberant banquets, melancholy;
Comrade of songs and escapades,
Ideals and strivings, poetic, clever—
Out there in a crowd of kindred shades
His genius flows away forever.

So tighter, dear friends, draw the ranks
Of the faithful. And now that I've finished
This song for the dead, let's give thanks,
And salute vital hopes, undiminished.
For the hopes of our Lyceum days
Are alive with us now at the feast.
Let's embrace one another and praise
Their principled lives, not deceased.

Moment's silence after poem.

Pushkin. Well, to work. Danzas, sincere thanks for your support. But I also feel guilty dragging you into this. Duels are illegal. There could be a mess if the authorities get word. For my part I've tried to keep it a secret; but one way or another the affair must be settled today, the day after the challenge.

Danzas. I've just met with D'Anthès' second at the French Embassy. Conditions are set. I have them.

Pushkin. Let's hear.

Danzas. Twenty paces. Each adversary five paces behind his barrier—the barriers ten apart.

Pushkin. Good. Pointblank. Bloodier the better.

Danzas. Pistols. At the signal, move forward—but not beyond the barrier. And fire.

Pushkin. Excellent. Watch, the coward will fire first: before he gets to the barrier.

Danzas. Once a shot is fired then neither of you must move. So the other's shot will come from the same distance.

Pushkin. Good. And then? What if we both miss?

Danzas. Start over. Same stipulations.

Pushkin. With pleasure. This duel won't end up in a marriage bed.

Danzas (reads). 'The seconds are intermediaries for any communications between duellists on the field of battle.'

Pushkin. Fine, Danzas. But you didn't say where.

Danzas. Beyond the Commander's Villa, near Black River.

Pushkin. Alright, listen. I'll bathe and put on clean linen. You go to Kurakin's, the gunsmith. I've ordered pistols. Hire a two-horse sleigh for the ride out to Black River. I'll meet you on Nevsky Prospect, at Wolf's sweet shop for a lemonade. Then we'll take the Troitsky Bridge out to the site . . . and get this sorry business over with.

Exit Danzas.

Pushkin (alone). Hm. So calm, happy almost . . . humming a tune since I woke up. It was the first sound night's sleep in a long time. Now with a sort of joy my silver watch goes on ticking, ticking in my pocket. Outside it's a cold winter day: wind whipping off the river. In here, warm. The gold light is on my bookcases. Daylight invites to a long life of productive work: great works to be written, a new phase. Now it's a middle period for Pushkin the poet—a richer realism, more movemented, dialectical like my *Dubrovsky* novel which has no hope to pass the censor. Works classical of form, modern for the content . . . What? No more time? Then I've made a beginning, for us.

Moment's silence.
He recites 'Exegi monumentum'.

> I've raised a monument not built by human hand—
> To myself. No weeds impede the people's path to
>   where
> It lifts up its rebellious head. And here I'll stand,
>   An Alexander's pillar in midair.
>
> No, I won't die entirely—spirit in sacred lyre
> Can outlast death, and will escape the rot and mould.
> And I'll be honored: long as there's a poet here
>   Fighting for truth, and principled, and bold.

Across great Russia go the rumors of my fate;
In every tongue and dialect they say my name—
Proud Slav's grandchild; and Finn; Tungus in savage
    state,
    Steppe-loving Kalmuck. They convey my fame.

And for a long, long time, our people will love me,
Since my work stirred and wakened thoughts of
    human goodness.
To this cruel age I sang. I eulogized the Free;
    Cried mercy for the oppressed; taught kindness.

O Muse, divinely mandated, go your faithful way,
Not shying from offenses, not striving after a wreath,
But slander and praise receiving with the news of the
    day—
    And with imbeciles saving your breath.

Pushkin stands frozen a moment.
Then he turns and goes out.

Gradually the natural light dims.
Thoughtful music: Beethoven piano sonata.
We hear lighthearted voices in the corridor: Natalya coming in from
a shopping spree.
More of the music. Time passing . . .

NIKITA KOZLOV, *the old valet, comes in the empty drawing room.*
Nikita (talks to himself). I'll light the lamps after awhile.
Pushkin will be home soon.
He exits.
We hear the three sisters fussing over ball preparations. Beethoven
segues to a light dance music.
This scene, as the three women tend to their toilette and fashions of
the day, is played like a dance number. NATALYA, EKATERINA *and*
ALEXANDRA *are the three Fates in a homely ballet.*

Natalya.

Let's get ready: pin my dress! For the ball!
Tonight I'll be the belle; j'suis tellement chic!
Nobles, generals, sophisticated gapers,
J'enchanterai le corps diplomatique.
Ah! There's Russia's foremost beauty at her capers,
And Tsar Nicholas outstares them all.

Ekaterina (lilting).

Like a diadem on the Neva Quay:
The bright red-carpeted front entry.
Armorial carriages, titled flor and fauna
In cordoned uniforms, ermine and satin: gentry
Sigh as she alights, Perugino's Madonna.
Gendarmes, liveried servants form a runway.

Natalya.

Lilac gowns with white barège
Trimmings, open collars, roses, bows,
Goosebumps! flushed perfumed skin—

Alexandra.

And now he appears, fashionable fop,
Male ogled wherever he goes,
And he flirts, and butts his pretty head in—

Ekaterina.

                    Stop,
Alexandra. Do not insult D'Anthès!

Alexandra.

Suffer, Pushkin, sulk.

Ekaterina.

> A more tender
> And charming man, more graceful dancer
> We won't see in many a season.

Alexandra.

> D'Anthès is a pest, a fatuous prancer
> Whose persistence is two-fold treason.

Natalya.

> Ouch! Too tight!

Ekaterina.

> You're not as slender.

Natalya.

> All day since noontime I've flurried about—
> At my magic toilette. Get it right!
> Bathed, powdered, perfumed, coiffeured à la
>   Grèque;
> Ribbons, pins; take up skirt; bust too tight!
> While my sisters wrangle like Abimelech:
> Bicker, trade insults, argue, pout.

Alexandra.

> If you showed such zeal for housekeeping! . . .
> But no; and so a genius spends his days
> On accounts, furnishings, domestics, équipage,
> Prosaic details. Debts mount. You play, he pays.
> While you astound the world with your
>   décolletage,
> Pushkin broods, can't write. With such sowing,
>   what reaping?

You yearn to see D'Anthès, tonight, again;
You pant for a coxcomb's flirtation.
Intoxicated by his insolence—
As men flock round, eyes wide with . . . admiration,
And call you 'Psyche', your beauty, charms
    'immense':
You lose your wits—can't end what you begin.

Ekaterina.

Shame! D'Anthès is my man. He's not for you.

Natalya (happy).

We'll let him pine and worship from afar.

Ekaterina.

Don't flutter your eyes at me, you witch. I know—

Alexandra.

What a pair! Both starry-eyed for a vain hussar.

Natalya.

I'll enjoy this ball tonight. Otherwise, why go?

Alexandra.

Why humiliate your husband? Play false for true?

Natalya.

At Razumovskys or the Karamzins
I turn a dress ball into madding rapture.
Tsar Nicholas can't keep his eyes off me.
In mazurka heaven I reign supreme; I capture
Men's flighty hearts, while women, enviously,
Gaze in a mass of diaphanous pinks and greens.

Alexandra.

And the great writer, public figure, on a dance floor
Looks ridiculous amid aristocratic youth
Who laugh at him—like them made by Nicholas
A Gentleman of the Chamber: insult to talent and
    the truth.
But Tsar wants Natasha for his quadrille at the
    Palace
Off-limits to a Foreign Ministry Titular Counselor,

Pushkin's prior rank. And so the poet, rheumatic,
Face bilious, lined with bitterness, no courtier
But a proud man humbled in a plumed tricorne
Follows his childish wife, the beauty, wherever her
Caprice leads: balls, masquerades, promenades,
    night till morn-
Ing, as the page boy falls afoul, erratic

As to dress: round hat? three-cornered? frock?
His gold buttons don't comply with official norms!
Or Pushkin plays truant. The Court notices, frowns
At his misbehavior. Days, weeks pass. He forms
Literary projects to pay for his wife's gowns.
Deeper in debt he yearns to work, and can't. The
    clock

Ticks. Months pass. Not family life, normal marriage,
But a circus! The author of *Godunov* bows, a menial,
And cuts a comic figure at Court balls;
Does obeisance to a Tsar who's uncongenial
To nonconformism. A lampoon appears. Prestige
    falls.
Slandered, blamed for his frivolous wife's
    miscarriage,

Surrounded by hostility, in increasing isolation,
Termed by young writers: court lackey, reactionary;
While enemies say his wife lost her child
Because he, the Othello she chose to marry,

Beat her up in a fit of rage, made wild,
Like a jealous devil, by her flirtation—

*In the background a carriage is pulling up outside. There are first
sounds of commotion: men's voices.*

*Alexandra goes on, as Natasha and Kati continue to primp and
preen the way they have done all through the scene.*

Alexandra.

I heard a scandalmonger say the other day
That just as Natalya's father went insane—
So will Pushkin, if this goes on much longer.
Society calls him peevish, a woman's bane,
Says he means to control, abuse her, wrong her—

Pushkin (with a groan that is shocking). Does it make you sad,
Nikita, carrying me this way?

*They come in led by Danzas whose clothes are streaked with red, as
are Pushkin's—carried in the arms of Nikita Kozlov.*

Danzas. Ready the divan for him in his study.

Ekaterina (hand to her brow; frowns, cries out). Ah! Where is my
husband? Where is George?

*Natalya (features contorted; throws up her arms; her response is
loud, hysterical, with a histrionic note).* Pushkin! Are you hurt?
Where have you been? What have you done?! You're bloody!
Look at all the blood!!

Danzas. He has been injured in a duel with D'Anthès.

Natalya. Oh-h-h-h! *(Hands to her head.)* Is it serious? Let me
see! I— Let me tend to my husband! I want to look after him!

Pushkin (weakly). Don't be alarmed. It isn't serious. Get me
clean linen.

*They move past her. Pushkin stares up at his wife who is pale, di-
shevelled, suddenly not beautiful.*

Natalya. Pushkin, the blood! The blood!

She screams, faints.

*Lights dim, as the day darkens toward evening. The drawing room
has emptied.*

*Low, dissonant music. Stirrings in the apartment—as they get
Pushkin settled in, and tend to Natalya.*

*Into the shadowy room, with a reddish purple twilight in the win-
dow, comes Nikita Kozlov seeing to the lights.*

A moment later a group enters. Alexandra and Danzas usher in
ZHUKOVSKY *and* TURGENEV.

Alexandra (not loud). Mr. Danzas, will you please tell us what
this is about?

Zhukovsky. What has happened?

Danzas. There's been a duel with D'Anthès. I was Pushkin's
second.

Turgenev. Where?

Danzas. At Black River, Mr. Turgenev.

Alexandra. Will you just tell us what happened?

Pause.

Danzas. . . . On the way out there, along the Palace Quay a
sleigh came toward us, and I saw it was his wife. I thought Natalya Nikolaevna might see us, but she's nearsighted as you
know. And Pushkin turned his head away.

Zhukovsky. He wanted this.

Turgenev. Yes, a resolution.

Danzas. He seemed pleased, even happy as our carriage trot-
ted through the streets filled with people enjoying the winter
day. Petersburg society was returning from the hills, skating and
tobogganing. Pushkin waved to them and chatted about his
younger days when duels were in fashion. The Cricket as we
called him then, in school, had a duel with Küchelbecker the
Lyceum comrade he loved so. He wouldn't shoot and said his
gun was loaded with cranberries. Another time, duelling a military man he thought cheated him at cards, the Cricket ate cher-
ries as he waited to be shot at . . . and then shrugged and left the
field.

Zhukovsky. I wonder if he ever shot to kill.

Turgenev. And this time?

Danzas. On the Kammenostrovsky Prospect two Horse
Guard officers passed us. One, Prince Golitsyn, called: 'Why're
you going out so late? Everybody's coming back!' . . . Along the

quay Pushkin laughed and asked if I was taking him to the
Petropavlosk Fortress. No, I told him, it's the quickest way to
Black River. The fortress looked somber out there by the frozen
Neva. An icy wind cut in off the sea. But he looked happy and
cried, 'Ah! There's Count Borkh. His name signed the anonymous letter, my cuckold diploma! He and his wife are a model
pair: she cohabits with the coachman, he with the post-boy . . .' I
thought there was something terrible about Pushkin then, so
happy with his Count Borkh, as reddish snowflakes lit on his
side whiskers, and his breath congealed.

Lips pressed, Danzas bows, shakes his head a little.

Turgenev. And then?

Danzas. And then, Mr. Turgenev, in a grove near the Commander's Villa I trampled snow, preparing the terrain with
D'Anthès' second. Pushkin sat on a snowdrift watching as we
laid our overcoats for barriers ten paces apart. 'Is it alright?' I
asked. And he shrugged: 'Just do it quickly.' As we loaded the
pistols he said: 'Well, have you finished?'

Turgenev. And D'Anthès?

Danzas. He stood there, looking on. His beaver collar framed
his arrogant pretty face. His overcoat was open on his white
Horse Guards uniform.

Alexandra. And then?

Danzas. Then we were ready . . .

Pause.

Zhukovsky. Go on.

Danzas. When they were in place, I waved my hat as the signal to begin. Pushkin moved toward the barrier. D'Anthès . . .

Danzas pauses again; considers something.

Turgenev. What then?

Danzas. D'Anthès took four steps forward. After a few seconds a shot rang out. Pushkin said, falling: 'I'm hit'.

Alexandra (eager). Was it fair, Danzas?

Danzas. The understanding is to reach the barrier and then
fire. D'Anthès is an officer and knows this. But he shot before arriving while Pushkin was kept from firing by his sense of honor.

Alexandra. Oh.

Turgenev. Honor. While they hound him to death. Worry the
life out of him. Honor.

Alexandra. Where were the police? Didn't Benkendorf know
about this? Duelling is illegal.

Zhukovsky. He knew. Heeckeren was at Stroganovs asking for advice . . .

Turgenev. They knew, and sent the gendarmes elsewhere. The idea was to get rid of Pushkin.

Alexandra (softly). What then, Mr. Danzas?

Danzas. Then he fell on my overcoat serving as barrier. He didn't move, head in the snow. Pistol stuck in the snow, muzzle filled with it. Both of us seconds went toward him, and D'Anthès was leaving his position. But Pushkin propped up on his left hand and said: 'Hold on, I feel strong enough to take my shot'.

Alexandra. Did he?

Danzas. D'Anthès resumed his place. Stood sideways shielding his chest with his right arm. I gave Pushkin a clean pistol. Holding himself up he took aim, a long moment, fired. D'Anthès tottered, fell.

Alexandra. Was he killed?

Danzas. Pushkin tossed up his gun. 'Bravo!' he cried . . . It was over.

Zhukovsky. But the result, man.

Danzas. Pushkin seriously wounded. Thought his thigh was shattered as blood flowed on the snow. Almost fainted, mind confused, but since then he's been lucid. He said: 'Did I kill him?' I said D'Anthès was wounded in the arm and chest. He said it was strange, he thought it would give him pleasure to kill this man, but now he didn't feel that.

Alexandra. How serious? Pushkin so bloody: he's lost a lot of blood.

Danzas. He was bleeding. And it wasn't easy bringing the sleigh to the clearing. Then the slow ride home began, bounced and jostled, but he didn't complain. By the Commander's Villa was a closed carriage sent by Heeckeren. I said yes when D'Anthès offered it, but I didn't tell Pushkin. I rejected D'Anthès' request to keep his part in the duel a secret.

Zhukovsky. So he was okay. On his feet.

Danzas. Yes.

Alexandra. But now begins to think what he's done.

Turgenev. Used as a tool. To destroy Russia's great writer.

Zhukovsky. Foreigner.

Danzas. On the way here Pushkin said tell his wife this isn't serious. He mentioned Sherbatov wounded fatally in the abdomen during a duel. Then pain and nausea came over him. He was quiet. By then we saw the lights of the city. Heard the jingle of sleigh bells, people talking in the street.

Alexandra. They poisoned his life. Now destroyed him, maybe. But they gave him a nice carriage to come home in.

Danzas. There's blood all over it.

AT NESSELRODES

Voices, laughter. Clink of champagne glasses.

Applause as D'ANTHÈS *enters in his white uniform, arm in a sling. On one side of D'Anthès is* BARON HEECKEREN, *on the other* EKATERINA.

On hand are Pushkin's enemies: NESSELRODES, STROGA-NOVS, FIKELMONS, GRAND DUKE MIKHAIL, COUNT UVAROV, COUNT URUSOV, PRINCE DOLGORUKOV, PRINCE GAGARIN, PRINCESS BYELOSELSKAYA, PRINCE TRUBETSKOY, COUNT BENKENDORF.

Byeloselskaya. Hail to the conqueror!

Urusov. A hero of our time!

Trubetskoy. Friend of Russia.

Heeckeren. Dear Friends . . . *(They grow quiet as he makes a statement.)* We are so grateful to you all. In these trying hours your faith and support touches our hearts. My son George and I won't forget it.

Uvarov. Count on us, Baron.

Dolgorukov. Hear hear!

Heeckeren. A long line of carriages has formed outside the Dutch Embassy, bringing us the warmth of true friendship, the encouragement of well-wishers. Petersburg society has come out for us tonight. This means so much to George and Ekaterina forced to go through such an ordeal on the threshold of their marriage and family life together.

Dolgorukov. Long and happy life to them.

Countess Nesselrode. George deserves happiness.

Trubetskoy. He deserves a monument!

Gagarin. I hear Pushkin's condition is serious. He could die.

Grand Duke Mikhail. Well then, good riddance.

Scattered laughter.

Benkendorf. We must be vigilant. There are signs of anger stirring as word of this reaches the people. There is grumbling among our Third Estate, intelligentsia such as it is and artists, civil servants, merchants. Pushkin for all his airs and insistence on nobility is a sort of leader to these elements.

Uvarov. As Minister of Education I am forbidding any demonstrations. No pro-Pushkin activities on our campuses. And should he die I will not permit professors and students to leave their classes for the funeral.

Benkendorf. Already there are people in the streets.

Countess Nesselrode. If he dies it will be his own fault. His hubris. He insulted and provoked both George and Baron Heeckeren in the most vulgar, shocking way.

Stroganov. Conceited little man: he was spoiled by success. Forever being told he's a classic.

Countess Nesselrode (looks fondly at D'Anthès). George's behavior has in all respects been that of a man of honor.

Urusov. Beyond reproach!

Dolgorukov. There's talk the poet may be dying, going into his agony. It seems he asked for his forgiveness to be conveyed to George D'Anthès. What do you say to that, Sir?

D'Anthès (laughs easily). Well, I forgive him too.

Countess Nesselrode. Can you give us a word or two about what happened?

D'Anthès. Eh bien . . . I hope he pulls through. I didn't mean to kill him. When I saw the face he made, so filled with hate and desire to hurt me, I shot first. Judge me who will.

Countess Nesselrode. No one is judging you.

Uvarov. On the contrary!

Dolgorukov. We admire you!

D'Anthès. I did all I could to make peace with him. But he insisted. And then came disgusting insults. On the terrain I saw my own death written in his eyes, so my reflex was to fire after four steps of the five marked off to the barrier. I aimed at his leg but hit higher: maybe due to my fear at the look of him.

Pause.

Countess Nesselrode. Of course.

Count Nesselrode. Now on his deathbed, if so it is, he must look after his wife and children's interests. Think of the debts he has made. Now you won't hear any sarcastic epigrams, his impertinence. The staggering debts must be paid, and who will do it?

Stroganov. Our benevolent Emperor.

Pause.

Benkendorf. So he will, Count Stroganov . . . Yet the people are coming out. We weren't expecting such repercussions.

Uvarov. I got an anonymous letter saying the innocent ones, Baron Heeckeren and George here, should be punished. But their so-called victim *(he sneers)* must be given a state funeral.

Byeloselskaya. What an idea.

Trubetskoy. Impudence is what it is.

Benkendorf. We'll forbid all obituary notices. We'll suppress his works, and begin by banning his play *The Covetous Knight* about to be premiered.

Uvarov. If not there could be a riot.

Benkendorf. Precisely. He's been a talented poet but an enemy of authority. The Emperor helped him time and again: did him one favor after the next. But Pushkin only pretended to mend his ways. Around him are grouped his supporters; they form a circle, and we know who they are. Now, if he does die, there'll be people flocking to see the body. We could have a violent mob on our hands, a deplorable spectacle, and triumph for the enemies of Russia.

Uvarov. This is why we're suppressing all honors.

Byeloselskaya (throws up her hands with a little cry). It's the Revolution! The ghost of Stenka Razin is on the warpath!

Laughter.

Benkendorf. We're taking measures.

Stroganov. I'll pay for the funeral. We'll control it.

Gagarin. I heard he has only 75 rubles to his name.

Uvarov. We'll make it a crime to buy his books.

Countess Nesselrode (softly). Let him die and be done with it. Put him out of his misery, and spare us the sight of him.

Grand Duke Mikhail. Good riddance.

Byeloselskaya. Long live Baron George D'Anthès Heeckeren!

Urusov. Long live D'Anthès the man of honor!

All Together (with applause and laughter). Long live! Vive l'Empereur! Long live Tsar Nicholas! Da zdravstvuyet!

NIGHT

PUSHKIN'S STUDY

DAHL, *a doctor who is also a writer, attends the wounded man.*

Pushkin. Doctor Dahl, what do you think of my situation?

Dahl. I can't hide from you that it's serious.

Pushkin. When I was hit, I felt a hard blow on the side, a burning pain in the loins. Lost a lot of blood. But tell me frankly: how is the wound?

Dahl. We'll know soon. The Emperor's physician has been sent for: let's wait for his opinion.

Knock on the door.

Natalya. Alexander Sergeyevich, let me come in.

Pushkin. No, don't enter. Dahl is here. *(To the doctor who is applying a new compress.)* I don't want her to see the wound. But I ask you again, Doctor: is it fatal?

Dahl. Duty compels me not to hide the danger.

Pushkin. Thank you for the truth. *(Hand to forehead; voice goes up a little.)* It seems I have some matters to tend to.

Dahl. Your close friends are here. Wouldn't you like to see them?

Pushkin (glances at books lining the walls, and gestures). Farewell, dear friends. Really I don't have an hour to live?

Dahl. I didn't mean that. But Mr. Zhukovsky is here. I thought it would be pleasant for you.

Pushkin. Well, well, so it's bad. Give me some water, Doctor, I'm nauseous. Ah, ah . . . Please don't hold out any false hopes to my wife; she's not an actress, she wants the truth . . . You know, I got an invitation to attend the funeral of Grech's son who died of consumption. It seems I won't be able. But if you see him, bow to him for me. Tell him I feel his loss with all my heart.

Dahl. I will.

Pushkin. I permit you to take all necessary steps, Doctor. I'm ready for anything.

Soft knock on the door. Dahl opens: it is the Tsar's physician, Arendt.

In low tones the two doctors confer a moment. Then Dahl goes out. Arendt, with a nod, nears the bed for a look at the wound.

Pushkin. Hello, Dr. Arendt. The Emperor is kind to send you here. How does it look?

Arendt (examining). The Emperor has sent you a letter.

Pushkin. Oh? Please read it to me.

Arendt (takes envelope from his vest; reads). 'If it is not God's will that we see each other again, then receive my farewell, along with my advice to die a Christian and take communion. As to your wife and children: have no fear. I will take care of them.'

Pushkin. May I keep the letter?

Arendt. No, I have orders to return it to His Majesty.

Pushkin. Please, Sir, ask Nicholas not to punish my second. Danzas should not be prosecuted for his part in the duel. Ah! *(He groans—features twisted.)* The pain . . . at moments. *(Voice quavers.)* I don't know if I can stand it. *(Turns head away, toward wall.)*

Arendt (lingers at the bedside a moment; then turns to go out. Leaving, he nods at Danzas posted outside the door, and says, low): It is a vile joke. He will die.

The door is closed quietly as, beyond it, the two men talk in low tones.

Pushkin (raises himself, gasping, on an elbow. He gropes with his free hand and produces a small revolver.) I'd end this right now . . . but I have debts that aren't written down. Make a list with Danzas, and then . . . Ei, ei, die a good Christian and the Tsar will 'take care of' my wife . . . All my adult life under their 'care'—sent into exile; letters opened; spies all around me thanks to that inbecile Benkendorf's surveillance. My own father they used as an informer; and then he said I threatened to kill him . . . *(He taps his temple with the gun.)* I'm drawn into debt by Nicky's need to see my wife at every ball; and then they won't let me publish my works to pay for it. *Bronze Horseman*— censored! *Dubrovsky*—hopeless! The devil had me born in this godforsaken country with talent and a conscience. I wanted to go see Europe; China with a delegation; the war in Turkey . . . No, no, no: it's the stinking cesspool of their court for me, and Benkendorf's meddling officiousness and bad faith. Envy, ill will, intrigues, spying, slander, balls, frivolity, debts, debts, debts! Let's all gang up on the poet Pushkin, ruin him, so we won't have to hear the truth anymore. Ha ha ha! *(Groans deeply.)* Ah-h-h. This pain . . . That's enough, I'll do it now. *(Points the gun at his head.)* But she'll hear the shot. She'll scream . . . *(Groans.)* I don't want them to hear me howling like a beast in a trap! Can't even die without playing a comedy . . . and getting letters from our beloved Tsar. I wish I could face the lying scoundrel at ten paces. Then I wouldn't muff it with my ridiculous sense of honor, waiting for a coldblooded killer to reach the barrier and shoot me down. Ah! Ah! I can't stand this anymore. That's it! Now I'll squeeze—

DANZAS comes in the room—sees what is happening. He lurches forward and grabs the pistol away.

Danzas (lips pressed; shakes his head a little). I'll challenge D'Anthès. He cheated with his four steps. They know it; and so they say I shouldn't have given you a fresh pistol. I'll avenge you.

Pushkin. No, Danzas. Nobody will avenge me. What you can do is keep my wife out of here. Where is she?

Danzas. In the drawing room.

Pushkin. Waiting to come in?

Danzas. N-no. Sleeping.

Pushkin. Good. I never was the handsome gallant she wanted. But no need to show her the poor devil: eyes popping out of their sockets with pain, forehead beaded with sweat, lips foaming. It'd only scare her. *(Weary gesture.)* She might think she was to blame for something. Ah! *(Grimaces.)* Ah, this—

Danzas. I'll go tell the doctor you have pain—and come right back.
Pushkin (tries not to holler). Oh! Oh! Maybe . . . it's better for my wife and children . . . if I die. Look how swollen it is. They tried to give me an enema, but the sacrum is shattered, the rectum so tumefied . . . any pressure makes me squawk.
Danzas. I'll go tell them.
Pushkin. Wait . . . You've been a faithful friend since our days as classmates. *(Takes off a ring.)* Please accept this, dear comrade. Keep it in memory of me. Ah! Ah! *(groans),* maybe they could drain the wound . . .?
Danzas, glancing back, goes out.
Pushkin is convulsed with pain.
Groans subside as he loses consciousness.

After a silence, music: the beginning ('Adagio, ma non troppo e molto espressivo') of Beethoven's 14th String Quartet.

First light in the window.
The string quartet blends into distant churchbells wafted over Saint Petersburg at dawn.
Pushkin (stirs). I feel less pain. *(Looks around.)* Night's almost over. Dawn soon. What for . . . the torture? I might've died in peace without upsetting people. An animal knows how to die, a tree.
NATALYA *bursts in with a cry. Now she doesn't look beautiful. She throws herself toward the bed—and kneels, kissing his hands.*
Pushkin (gives a little laugh, and recites).

> When I take your statuesque
> Body in my embrace,
> And in my rapture lavish
> Kisses, with some commonplace,
> Then wordless from my timid fingertips
> You ease your graceful form;
> There's a dubious grin on your lips,
> Dear friend, not yearning, loving, warm.
> For you know your husband's history,

All a past of sad betrayals;
And so, unsympathetically,
You look away . . . Nothing avails.
And then I curse the amorous cunning
Of my younger days: love's vow, lust's rite
When my next tender victim came running
To the silent garden at night.
Now I disavow such . . . intercourse,
Voluptuous verse to stir the nerves;
Caresses of gullible girls, and, of course,
Their tears, and belated murmurs.

He laughs low.

Natalya (weeping, head bowed). I'm sorry. I'm sorry.

Pushkin. Be quiet, you're not to blame. Anyway I feel much better. I'm going to live.

He strokes her head as she kneels by the bedside, crying.

Natalya. Oh, oh.

Pushkin. Remember . . . last February, the affair at Princess Butereau's. *(Pushkin closes his eyes.)* Liveried footmen lined the wide staircase as we arrived. Rare flowers, tropical plants in the luxurious rooms. The great hall with its gilded marble walls, like a temple of fire; it blazed. And there stands D'Anthès, chats, flirts: hero of the grand dress ball with his gaze that implores, his words more risquée than any Russian's. And the two of you danced, and looked madly in love, throwing caution to the winds.

Natalya. Don't . . . don't.

Pushkin. I should have put an end to it then. He troubled you, I know. Later you told me he proposed you become his mistress. And someone told me he said: 'This woman, you know, doesn't pass for the most intelligent . . .' And once you begged him: 'Please, Monsieur D'Anthès, take pity on my innocence. You have my heart, but the rest does not belong to me'.

Natalya (broken voice). How do you know that?

Pushkin. He'll tell the other scamps gathered round Heeckeren how he worships you, and *(mock sigh)* . . . 'what a terrible thing it is to love . . . and not say so except between two ritournelles of a contredanse'.

Natalya. Why didn't you tell me this?

Pushkin (weary gesture). How many times, how many ways. I should have taken you to the country.

Natalya. Yes, why didn't you?

Pushkin. You'd go into a pouting fit . . . Well, you're young and beautiful, you should rule. Plus you enlisted Ekaterina, your mother, who else, against me. *(Pause.)* The day we got married in Great Ascension Church . . . remember? The ring fell from my hand. Bad omens. No matter how hard I tried, I couldn't find the way to . . .

Natalya. No, no.

Pushkin (weary gesture). Now I want you to go out to the children. Bring them here. I want to see them. Go—

She goes out.
He recites.

It's time, my friend, high time. The heart says let it be.
Days pass, the clock tictocs, each hour as it flows by
Erodes a bit of being. Well, together, we
Proposed to live. And now see that? It's time to die.

What happiness on earth? To live in peace is sweet.
For a long time I've dreamed a home of warmth and
    light.
A long time, worn out slave, I've plotted my retreat
To some far place of work, fulfillment, pure delight.

The three small children are brought in. Sleepy, in pajamas, they look to Alexandra and Nikita Kozlov more than to their mother.

Behind them is Danzas who has been keeping watch in the doorway.

Pushkin. Bless you, Masha. Bless you, Sasha. Bless you, Natasha. *(He lies back, propped on cushions.)* Go back to bed, my children. Grow up strong, true, happy.

The three adults usher them out.

Natalya (cries from outside). He will live! I can feel it! I just know he won't die!

Silence.

In the other rooms we hear a coming and going. People are arriving. As the scene moves along the stir, also outside in the street, begins to build.

ZHUKOVSKY *comes in.*

Pushkin (weakly). O Zhukovsky, old comrade-in-arms. What's that I hear?

Zhukovsky. People.

Pushkin. Ah, so they're out there, living. But I'm in here. I think . . . the sadness is worse than the pain.

Zhukovsky. Dr. Arendt said in all his military campaigns he's seen little that compares with your suffering and courage.

Pushkin. Is my wife alright? Someone better stay with her.

Zhukovsky. Don't worry.

Pushkin. Or . . . could you have her come in? You know, I . . . would like her to feed me . . . some raspberries.

Zhukovsky goes to the door and gives Danzas the order.

Pushkin. What's the noise I hear?

Zhukovsky. There are people here. The foyer is filled with friends. And outside the house a crowd is gathering.

Pushkin. Why?

Zhukovsky. Why? *(Small laugh.)* Because genius is for the good of us all. All the peoples are united in their love of it.

Pushkin. So, so. Success was my tragic flaw. Without it they'd have left me alone. Then I would've done something.

Zhukovsky. We all share your pain, we feel brotherly grief. What you've done isn't only for Russia, but for humanity.

Pushkin. Sounds like a lot of them out there.

Zhukovsky. A lot.

Pushkin. Too bad, isn't it? . . . Doesn't matter what the doctors do: apply leeches—I helped them!—and ice packs to keep the fever down. Seems there's no place for me here. It's clear; it seems necessary. Oh, I could have written the broad river of Russian life . . . a Homer of our time . . . to enlighten our people: make them proud, give them courage, honor.

Zhukovsky. We still have hope.

Pushkin. Who's outside among our friends? Can I see them? Have them come in. And, Zhukovsky, this gold chain and cross . . . please see that my sister-in-law Alexandra gets it, so that she . . . I haven't wanted her to come in here. You see, I . . . Please make sure she gets it.

* * * * *

One by one the close friends come in.* TURGENEV, MADAME KARAMZIN, PRINCE VYAZEMSKY, PRINCE ODOEVSKY, COUNT VYELGORSKY, DANZAS, DR. DAHL. *They take up positions by the bed.*

Pushkin. Farewell, Vyazemsky, friend *(presses his hand),* be happy. *(Embraces Turgenev.)* Turgenev, dear comrade, I love you . . . all of you . . . *(His voice breaks. Then to Madame Karamzin.)* It would mean so much . . . if you would bless me.

Karamzin (broken voice). Bless you.

Pushkin (overcome by pain, gasps). How long does this foolishness . . . ah!

Natalya comes in. Features pale, impassive, thick chestnut hair down over her shoulders, she kneels by the bed. Cheek to cheek, she feeds him raspberries with her fingers.

Pushkin. So good . . . they taste . . . like my childhood. Like the ones my nurse, Arina Rodionovna . . . what I owe that good woman . . . what our literature owes her, for the folktales she told me, stories and fairy tales with a heart . . . like she had. Birds were chirping in the trees outside . . . sweet smell of grass and sunlight across the meadow, down to the river . . . at Mikhailovskoye while I was in exile, writing and studying . . . Arina's preserves were stewing in a copper pot. And then strolling among the muzhiks' huts, visiting with them . . . talking, joking, joining in their songs. Or I went to the monastery dressed up in a straw hat and peasant shirt . . . hair wild, bearded after my days and nights of work . . . and I sang on the steps in the crowd of beggars . . . Well, well, little wife, don't cry now . . . Be brave. Try to be forgotten. Go live in the country. Stay in mourning for two years and then remarry . . . Choose a decent man.

Natalya. No, no.

Pushkin (stroking her head). You see? It is nothing . . . there, there. Everything has turned out for the best.

Natalya. You won't die. You will live.

Pushkin. I feel dizzy . . . like I was climbing up high, so high . . . over those bookcases. My head is turning.

---

*Pletnyev, the poet's close friend and publisher, is edited out for the sake of concentration.

Dr. Dahl (low). The end is coming.
Pushkin (recites, his voice like a flickering candle).

> All in her is wonder, harmony;
> No vanity or anger, never spiteful, regretful;
> All in her is placid . . . modesty,
> Victoriously beautiful.
> She casts a statue's classic glance
> And spies no rival, has no friends.
> Pale mortal beauties prance and may entrance;
> She keeps her chill magnificence.

(Weakly.)

> Wherever you were scurrying,
> To your destiny . . . a lover's tryst,
> What ever your heart was cherishing,
> Diamond, star ruby, amethyst:
> Crossing her path in confusion you
> Pause in a trance, gaze worshipful
> At divinity demanding its due,
> Imperiously beautiful . . .

Voices are heard from outside.
1st Voice. What's happening? Is he better?
2nd Voice. Is he still alive?
3rd Voice. Is his wife with him? Has he forgiven her?
4th Voice. Is her lover, the Frenchman, still in the city?
1st Voice. That murderer, he'd better get out!
5th Voice. I've heard the Tsar—
2nd Voice. Has there been a statement?
6th Voice. Is there still hope? Will Pushkin live?
Child's Voice. I hope he lives!

Dahl (low). He is going.
Moment of silence.
Pushkin (erupts). Raise me up! Higher! Well, come on, higher!
. . . I can't breathe . . . Where's Turgenev? Give me your hand, al-

right, let's go then . . . but, please, together . . . *(Pushkin's eyes open wide. His face brightens, clears of pain.)* Life is over.
A shiver runs through his arms, extremities.
Silence.
Natalya. Pushkin! Are you living? Pushkin! Pushkin! *(Sobs.)*

Lights dim slowly.
Zhukovsky (his voice over Natalya's subsiding sobs—seems to disengage from the scene—more distantly—as if writing, eulogizing). Look at his face in the first moments of death. So new . . . yet I've known it forever. It isn't sleep, and not peace . . . as his hands come to rest after a heavy task. It isn't wit, the intelligence so innate to his features. No. But a profound, an astonishing thought plays over them now, like a vision . . . *(Outside, the crowd voices gather, grow louder. In here the lights dim further.)* . . . some complete, deep, gratifying knowledge, come over his features. What is it you see? What would you say if you could speak now? Tell death itself? . . . *(His voice blends in with the crowd noise on the rise: people calling out, questions, the note of protest, street sounds. Lights down.)* I swear to you I never saw such a profound, great, triumphant look on the face of a man. It was there at instants during his life: refracted by his struggles. But now, look! Such a purity, in contact with death. So this is how you end . . .

Sounds of a big crowd in movement, in the street. They carry over to the next scene.

ROYAL STABLES CHURCH

Night. Crowd with torches: flickering light. It is the street outside, as Pushkin's funeral service goes on inside. Through this scene we have the crowd with us, voices, background noises; also organ and other church music comes wafting.

The people express their grief. Some weep.

Held high are copies of a new portrait of the poet, edged in black, with the words: 'The fire has gone out at the altar'.

Nobles jostle among the masses. All are excited.

An OLD MAN *is weeping.*

Turgenev. Why are you crying? You knew Pushkin personally, no doubt?

Old Man. No, but I am Russian.

Odoevsky (to Turgenev, Rosset, Zhukovsky, Vyazemsky). The Chairman of the Board of Censors called me to his office. He said the Minister is upset over my obituary* in the literary supplement. 'What, sir, do you mean by saying: The sun of our poetry has set . . . ?'

As people in the crowd turn to listen, the spirited Alexandra Rosset (Smirnova) reads from the obituary.

Organ music from church in background.

Rosset. I have it here. *(Raising her voice.)* 'Pushkin is dead— dead in the prime of his magnificent career!' *(Crowd response: groan, cries.)* 'We haven't the strength to say more. And besides: why try? Every Russian heart knows what this loss means to us, and is torn by it. Pushkin! Joy and glory of our people! Is this really happening? We cannot accept it!'

STUDENT. Down with the assassin!

COACHMAN. Down with the foreigner who killed our pride and joy!

WOMAN IN HEAD SCARF. Pushkin, my son, my shining one: what did they do to you?

SOLDIER WITH WAR MEDAL. What have they done? Let them account for this!

Turgenev. Out here the people are stirred up like a surging sea. In there lies Pushkin with his enemies, the aristocrats and Ministers of State, Nesselrodes and Stroganov—who is paying for the funeral so it would be like this—and the Uvarovs, Urusovs, Fikelmons, Benkendorf the Police Chief and all the other cronies of the throne. And they're afraid.

Music. The three-part canon of Archbishop Andrew of Crete is heard from the church.

Odoevsky. Afraid of a ghost! And in a huff! I hear the Emperor

---

*Kraevsky, in reality, wrote the obituary.

is vexed with us for dressing our dear friend in civilian clothes, and not his official uniform—so he could be a Gentleman of the Bedchamber for all eternity in his coffin lined with purple velvet.

Vyazemsky. I sent a note to Grand Duke Mikhail asking why Benkendorf had his spies at the dead man's home: eavesdropping on our grief and tears.

Student (cries). Why aren't they honoring him with a state funeral? Why skulk over here to Stable Street at midnight? as if they meant to hide their shame, and separate the great writer from the people?!

MERCHANT. That can't be done!

SERVANT GIRL. Пушкин! Добрый! . . . молодец!*

CHILD. Молодец!

Odoevsky. During my meeting with the censor, Uvarov said: 'Was Pushkin a general? a Minister of State? a statesman?'

Turgenev. All of them, the Uvarovs and Trubetskoys, the Stroganovs and Nesselrodes are in there: inside the church with their official grief put on like decorations.

Rosset. All the courtiers, ambassadors, princesses—in white gloves and high headdresses and lorgnettes!

Odoevsky. But they're worried. I think a little spooked!

Turgenev. For three days thousands and thousands of our people passed by the coffin of this man become in death more than a writer—in fact a national symbol.

Rosset. Symbol of our dignity. Of our will as a people to be free.

Vyazemsky. That's why they send spies. They're here too and everywhere listening, reporting.

Danzas (joining them). Dear friends! Look how they cancelled the public funeral service which was supposed to be celebrated at 11 a.m. at Cathedral of Saint Isaac!

Turgenev. In broad daylight.

Rosset. They knew the people's love would shine out before the eyes of the world!

Turgenev. And the people's anger.

Zhukovsky. Natalya had invitations sent out for it. But the Archbishop refused to officiate.

Music. Crowd noise. Torches.

Rosset (voice raised). And so they have us come here in the

---

*Pushkin! Kind! . . . Brave one!

dark—with our torches following his mortal remains. And the police follow alongside us. I tell you I lower my head in shame now: not for myself but for the Tsar and for Russia!

Organ notes from inside the church.

2nd SOLDIER. Why am I here? Why did they send me?

3rd SOLDIER. Is this a war? General Dubelt went with twenty officers to remove the body!

Soldier with War Medal. They haven't forgotten December!

Odoevsky. They thought public services might be the signal for some organized action: a popular outcry, even an insurgency!

1st WORKER. I heard there were death threats against the foreigners who killed him.

OLD WOMAN. And against his wife, the slut!

Woman in Head Scarf. Is she here?

2nd WORKER. In there with his enemies!

2nd Soldier. All rejoicing in his death while they give him the ritual kiss.

Coachman. Well then I hope they enjoy the taste.

Old Woman. The black slime on his lips! I saw it when my Matveï died.

Servant Girl. Пушкин! добренкыи!

Danzas. While they snip locks of hair and snatch off buttons as souvenirs.

Turgenev. Tear away a patch of his coat: his 'lucky coat' we dressed him in—

Zhukovsky. The one a friend lent him seven years ago when he became engaged to Natalya.

Child. Молодец! Я люблю вас!*

Choral strains from 'Sky and Earth'—Ukrainian vesper.

WOMAN'S VOICE (*people look around: where is she?*). Look! comrades, don't you see what's happening? Benkendorf and the forces of order planned this with the Tsar's benediction! When D'Anthès came on the scene they saw their chance! It's like French revolutionaries provoked into duels during the Great Revolution!

Merchant. Now his books are selling like crazy in the bookstores! They said he was finished, but Smirdin has taken in 40 thousand rubles in two days!

---

*Brave one! I love you!

Zhukovsky. That's true. You can't find the new edition of
Yevgeny Onyegin anywhere.

*Out of the crowd noise, talk, cries and murmurings, like an amor-
phous chant with organ notes—a solo voice emerges. It is* MAD
CHAADAEV *reciting Pushkin's 'The Dagger'.*

*As he moves through the stanzas the crowd noise recedes with the
music.*

*And then he is joined by other voices, including the Child's, Stu-
dent's, Women's, Workers' and Soldiers'—more and more voices until
all are chanting the final stanzas of 'The Dagger':*

Chaadaev:

> Hammered out in Lemnos at the forge of Vulcan,
> Chastizing dagger, secret sentry of Freedom:
> In the deathless hand of fated Retribution
> You oust arrogant usurpers, change regimes of scum.
>
> Zeus' thunder grows quiet? The law's sword is sleepy?
> Then you, like a missionary from the Devil,
> Slip in beneath the imperial canopy;
> And soon, amid the festive glitter, you too will revel.
>
> Bright flash out of hell, or god's lightning,
> The silent blade glints in the bandit king's eyes,
> As he glances about. There's something frightening
> In this carousal of power, like a banquet of spies.
>
> No matter where he goes, far travels, inside a church,
> Or in an army camp: you're there, O guillotine
> Waiting on history's nod. The victim gives a lurch,
> The bloody thrust strikes home. Revenge is now, on the
>   scene.
>
> Beneath great Caesar's gaze the sacred Rubicon
> Flows on. Sovereign Rome falls. The Law hangs its
>   head.

But Brutus rises up and strikes the tyrant down.
So much for despot rule. The bloody Tsar is dead.

Now the People's fury rages forth in a roaring storm,
The thunder and lightning of revolt roar through the
　　land.
Now over martyred Freedom, over its headless form
Stands the monstrous executioner, dagger in hand.

Apostle of death he'll test the capacity of Hell
As he gathers with a tap the criminals of state.
He was sent by a higher court to ring the joyous knell,
Sent hand in hand with a Eumenid by a judge named
　　Fate.

Justice is a student chosen of destiny,
Young fighter who has to die on the hangman's
　　scaffold.
But the sacred benefactor lives in History.
Martyrs' dust has a way of speaking. Truth gets told.

Truth is a ghost that roams the homeland eternally.
Let the oppressors lie, swindle, kill. Let them swagger.
On the principled militant's grave, trophy of victory,
Will burn without inscription the avenging dagger.

The people cheer, like a peal of thunder.
Vyelgorsky (approaches, joins the others). Dear friends! What a popular outpouring! It smells like rebellion in the air!
Turgenev. Does it? Always our people seemed to weep on cue from our dear little father the Tsar.
Rosset. There were times when even Pushkin in his anguish tried to do it.
Zhukovsky. His nature wouldn't let him.
Vyelgorsky. And now look! Out here the people are taking his cue. Tears of sadness and rage—and at the same time joy! There is something new going on here tonight.
Music: low at first, but a new note, chimes; an Easter Hymn from the Greek-Byzantine Liturgy.

Vyazemsky. Yes, we had our local revolts, Stenka Razin, Pugachev. This is national.

Odoevsky. The Third Estate comes out to honor its unofficial leader.

Danzas. There's muzhik dress in the crowd.

Vyazemsky. Workers, women, students, soldiers. One idea unites them tonight.

Rosset. Not divided! This is what frightens the Nesselrodes, the Benkendorfs, Uvarovs.

Vyelgorsky. Professors and students were told not to come. But they're here. And we're here. We like it better outside, it seems.

Crowd (like a groundswell, low at first). Push-kin . . . Push-kin . . . Push-kin!

Chaadaev (high voice riding above the crowd). Ei! One Pushkin died! Sacrificed to the enemy which destroyed him physically—first ruining him morally! Russia without a real history, Russia without a culture, Russia in denial, Russia not doing right! Ha ha ha! You can't tell the truth, but you can smell the truth! Another Pushkin lives on, a shining light! He has no tradition or precedent.

Crowd (louder). Push-kin . . . Push-kin . . . !

Zhukovsky. There's a rumor some people want to escort his convoy on foot—all the way to Pskov where he'll be buried. Said they'd take turns pulling the carriage in place of the horses.

Rosset. Who will escort it besides the police? Natalya Nikolaevna?

Zhukovsky. No, she's too exhausted and sick to take on that task. She asked the Emperor to let Danzas here go with the body.

Rosset. Will he?

Zhukovsky. Danzas is under arrest for his part in the duel, though left at liberty for the moment, as you see.

Rosset. Who then?

Zhukovsky. Turgenev . . . He'll go.

Vyazemsky. Look at all the students here from the university.

Vyelgorsky. That's an omen: when people refuse to obey a Government order.

Odoevsky. And are willing to face the consequences.

Danzas. How many were let inside?

Zhukovsky. Those with tickets or wearing an official uniform.

Turgenev (turns to the old woman who is dressed poorly and has tears in her eyes). Dear, take my ticket. Go in the church and keep warm.

Crowd (quite loud). Push-kin! Push-kin! Push-kin!

From inside the church waft sounds of high mass.
The choir sings: 'Come, brethren, give the departed a last kiss . . .'
Outside: the groundswell of chanting. Push-kin . . . ! Push-kin! . . .
Peasant. Here he comes now! See the footman in black?
Old Woman. Is he coming out?
Boy. I'll kill that D'Anthès myself!
Soldier with War Medal. We want to see the poet!
Woman with Head Scarf. Yes! Yes! Let us give him the final kiss!
Child. Молодец! Пушкин молодец!
Old Woman. Let us have our dear one!
Old Man. Голбчик наш.*

Zhukovsky. Who's suffering today? Is it the empty-headed doll who helped destroy him? No, it's Alexandra, his sister-in-law. She's the woman of so many in his life who loved him truly. Now she has a lifetime of grief ahead of her.

Turgenev. She, and the Russian people.

Crowd (one side). Farewell. Farewell, little master! Прощай! Прощай!

Chaadaev. You dog! Did you say Russia is a lying, denying madhouse? Did you fail to show the proper disdain for principle? the dignity of man? Did you say what had to be said?! . . . Then out, you dog! To Siberia with you—on the road of prehistory marked with the bones of the righteous!

Crowd (other side, roaring). Pushkin! Pushkin! Pushkin!

It all blends together in a crescendo. The chants and voices are joined with organ music and then the tolling of church bells.
Knell. Chants. Laments. Laughter. Cries.
Then this amazing 'music', church and crowd, voices, bells, fading chants—all gets lower. And over it comes Pushkin's voice reading his 'Elegy':

---

*Dear friend, dear lad.

Mad reckless years, the sounds of dying laughter
Weigh on me in the anxious morning after.
Like wine the sadness of remembered days
Is strengthened with the coming on of age.
My way is dark. Toil, sorrow call to me,
Tossed like a bell buoy on a stormy sea.

But O, dear friends, I do not want to die.
I want to live, create and suffer. I
Know full well there's more joy, love, jubilation
Amid life's cares, afflictions, agitation;
More times when I'll be drunk on harmony,
More tears run over for some poignant story;
And maybe—at the parting time, at sunset,
Love's farewell smile will shine—don't go, not yet!

Segue to peaceful clop-clop of a horse-drawn carriage along a road.

JOURNEY

Clop-clop of horses' hooves.
Slides are projected on the darkened stage—snowy scenery, the Russian countryside, southward to Mikhailovskoye in the province of Pskov.

Turgenev (reads from his journal). 'Yesterday, February 3rd, 1837, we set out. The Tsar asked me to go with Pushkin's body, nailed in a plain wood coffin, on its final journey.

'I looked back and saw Zhukovsky, standing in the moonlight, watching our procession of three troikas as it drew away from the church and out of sight.

'Twenty-six years ago I took the boy Pushkin to the Lyceum at Tsarskoye Selo, and saw him entered there . . .'

Slides change. Tsarskoye Selo, with park in springtime. Then Saint Petersburg gleaming in sunset.

Music from Musorgsky's Boris Godunov *begins to play low (Act III), and the swelling waves of lyricism accompany the narrative.* 'O, если б ты любил ее, Если б ты знал ее терзанья . . .'

'We set out. Benkendorf planned the journey to the last detail. It seems they fear Pushkin dead even more than alive . . .

'In the darkness of the Royal Stables Church crypt the poet lay waiting for us.

'A police officer climbed in the first troika.

'The coffin, tied with ropes and covered with tarpaulin, went in the second along with Nikita Kozlov, the poet's servant since childhood. Nikita came this way south when Pushkin was sent into exile. Now I see him up ahead, crouched beside the coffin, not moving despite the snow, wind and cold.

'I'm in the third carriage as we move through the Russian countryside and the night. *(Music; slide changes, etc.)* There is a frigid mist after the snow clouds pass. For now moonlight shimmers over the drifted snow, and the night is bright enough for me to write these lines.

'The horses move at a brisk pace across the Russian plains. At each station police are posted, and there are fresh horses. We can do 80 versts in a night. Why the hurry? There must be no popular outcry, no public display of grief. Guards stand by the coffin as we wait for harnessing.

'All his life they hindered his movements. Not so now. Bury me at Mikhailovskoye, he says, and it is expedited.

'Red hands, faces. Busy, stern. Military caps, icycled beards, mustaches. Official papers, stamps and seals, orders, salutes.

Slide of posting station, peasant faces.

'Just now we waited as policemen shouted at a stationmaster demanding fresh horses.

'Peasants stood staring at the sleigh and its wood box covered with straw. A woman asked them:

'—What's this?

'—God knows! It seems somebody shot Pushkin to death. And now they're speeding him away rolled up in a bast mat, under a heap of straw, like a dog.—

'On we roll through the moonlit night and the shining landscape.

'Moon and snow.

'February 4th. Night.

'The Governor here in Pskov has received a letter from Petersburg. There shall be no special events in honor of the poet: no receptions, ceremonies. The Emperor forbids it.

'February 5th. At one a.m. we set out by way of Ostrov for Trigorskoye where Pushkin is to be buried. We arrived here in midafternoon. The coffin with Nikita Kozlov and a mounted gendarme was sent on to Svyatogorsky, the Holy Mountain Monastery. I went to visit with Pushkin's friend during his exile here, Praskovya Osipova. She sent peasants to the monastery to dig the grave.

'February 6th. Last night we sat up late talking about him. We drank tea and looked over an old album. We recited his verses.

'In the house there are many memories: a silver jug used to make *djonka* for him after his traipses through the snow; the table where they sat talking and laughing together; the armchair by a frosted window where he liked to study.

'We remembered his noble brow and sparkling dark eyes so in love with life. The samovar steamed and whistled inside the snowbound old manor house. Was it possible he wouldn't come bursting in at any moment? Stamp his feet on the welcome mat and laugh happily—so radiant with life and intelligence it made everyone else happy?

'Before we knew it, we all sat there laughing together . . . But then, ah! He is gone.'

Surging music from Musorgsky's Boris Godunov, *Act III:* 'Но если, Димитрий, внушеньем божьим, Не отвергнет . . .' *It is a brief interlude—then continues beneath Turgenev's voice.*
Slides of Svyatogorsky Monastery.

'February 7th. Pushkin is buried. I left the same day. I am on my way home.

'At six in the morning I went to the monastery escorted by the police guard. Police, police—as in his life, so now in death, all around him.

'The steps were icy leading up to the monastery. A few muzhiks were working at the grave. Candles flickered in the window of a chapel.

'In the cold a priest hurried the mass, mumbling in his beard. Nikita Kozlov and the Mikhailovskoye peasants lowered Pushkin into the grave carved out of a bit of frozen earth filled with roots. We wept, and the tears froze on our cheeks. In early morning the red sun looked lonely, climbing into the pale expanse of winter sky. On the top of the monastery roof a few crosses threw off pink sparks in the sunrise. And then bells . . . The lonely church bells rang in the early morning hour.

'So the poet lies buried alongside his womenfolk. He is closer to his mother now than he was in real life. For she was a cold woman, and he married a cold one who was like her. Also buried there are his maternal grandmother and grandfather Hannibal.'

Slides of Pushkin's home, and surroundings; then interior, in Mikhailovskoye.
'Afterward I made a pilgrimage to Pushkin's home in Mikhailovskoye. The wide way in front was all white and bordered by tall snow-covered trees. The house, too, looked like a boat half-sunk in snow.

'A tearful caretaker unlocked the poet's study. By the window was a writing desk with a China inkwell, a quill pen. There were a few books: *Iliad,* Dante, Cervantes, Shakespeare. Now it was cold in this room where glories of our literature were created, *Onyegin, Godunov;* also the great folktales based on stories his old nurse Arina told him; and how many incomparable poems. Once it was warm in here—to warm the heart of humanity.

'Now cold, empty.

'The caretaker and his wife were crying.

'And so I am on the road home.

'We have left him back there alone. He is covered with the dark frozen earth and the snow.

'The wind blows with a moan over the lonely cemetery, over his grave.

'Spring will come.'

* * * * *

Music from Boris Godunov *surges, and fades.*
Slide of Pushkin's portrait.

First Witness. As for Pushkin: we watched him making himself ridiculous in every Petersburg drawing room. We saw his spite and hatred and thought him in quite bad taste. D'Anthès went about with charm and tact winning friends to his side even among the poet's adherents.

Second Witness. Pushkin had victory in his grasp, but he couldn't clinch it. And we didn't understand the situation. We condemned him since he wouldn't tell the reasons behind his behavior. He was honest, noble. He was good and simple, as he said, but his heart was sensitive.

Third Witness. How he must have suffered when I cordially shook hands with his enemy, the repulsive D'Anthès, in front of him. The honor of our Russian people was smeared by a foreign adventurer. And Pushkin's own countrymen, a small coterie that is, took up the fop's cause and demonized the great writer.

Fourth Witness. It was only after his death that we learned the truth about it, and about Heeckeren and D'Anthès. And we haven't seen those two rascals around here since. They were whisked away quick. Beyond the frontier they went, their job well done: as if that's the only reason they ever came here.

Fifth Witness. Lightly the cock struts about. And the whole sinister clique, the scandalmongers of fashion, thrive too ... Well, go ask Nesselrodes, and Police Chief Benkendorf; go ask Prince Dolgorukov who wrote the cuckold letter; go ask Tsar Nicholas—just what happened.

Sixth Witness. Cry! O my country with a curse on it. You will not soon give birth to another such son.

Slides: Pushkin portraits, scenes.
Then a simple grave in a churchyard.
Then a river, trees and fields, nature in springtime, as Alexandra's
voice reads from Yevgeny Onyegin.

Chased by the bright spring sunlight
Down surrounding hills the snow
Comes bounding in turbid streams
Already flooding the meadow.
The clear smile of nature gleams
As it greets the year sleepy-eyed
While the blue sky shines in its pride.
The still transparent woodlands
Are greening with a sallow down.
The bee leaves its wax hive and wends
Through the fields for its tax of pollen.
The valleys in bloom sparkle gaily.
Herds low toward pasture. A nightingale
Sang of spring in the silence last night.

Music, low, from Tchaikovsky's Yevgeny Onyegin, Act III: 'Он-
егин! Я тогда моложе, я лучше, кажется, была! И я любила вас
. . .'

How sad your advent is to me,
Springtime, springtime, season of love.
Nature stirs my depths with its listless kiss,
Enticing my heart, and my blood.
With what a voluptuous tenderness
I feel spring's warm breath on my face,
So at home in this peaceful place.
Or has pleasure become such a stranger—
Now all that rejoices, all that would live,
Expansive, free, affirmative
Brings only wan boredom, dull languour?

Nature plants its kiss on the living and dead
By this tomb where such life, such bustle led.
But the rest is gloom, obscurity.

Tucked in the rolling hills, not far from here,
There's a gurgling stream which roves
In a bend through a verdant field
To a river beyond some linden groves.
There the nightingale sings all night
Enamored of spring. There the wild rose blossoms
And a babbling brook gossips
All day long. On a humble headstone
In the shade of an age-old pine tree
The visitor reads an inscription:
'Here a young poet rests in eternity.
He died for honor, and without fear.
His age was not yet thirty-eight.
He was principled. He was great.'

Time was that an overhanging bough
In the early morning breeze
Seemed to lay a secretive wreath
Where a writer took his ease.
Sometimes, at dusk, after their workday
Two young women came here. The moon crept
Into the twilight at close of day.
The two friends embraced and wept.
Such was the melancholy monument
Of a young poet killed in a duel
In the prophetic epic *Onyegin*.

Slide of Pushkin's present-day gravesite.
Slide of Pushkin's monument.
Music from toward the end of Tchaikovsky's opera—Yevgeny
Onyegin.

History blights. Life finds renewal.
By the grave of Alexander Pushkin bow
And place this flower. All Russia comes here now.

1998-2008

Afterword:
Wherefore Tragedy?

Wherefore Tragedy?

'What element is unfolded in tragedy?
What is its aim? Man and the people.
The destiny of man, the destiny of the people.'

—*Pushkin*

If you ask a Russian who is that country's national writer: the name given is likely to be not one of the novelists, but Pushkin. Perhaps this has to do in part with distortions in the life and thought of Tolstoy and Dostoyevsky. Their creative work reflects the society and times with a richness of realism, profound psychology, magnificent panorama of life under Russian tsardom. But a clear and consequential analysis, a principled political position was a ticket to Siberia, as in the case of their contemporary Chernyshevsky. And so they drew back in a guise of religion. Despite the later Tolstoy's virulent and thoroughgoing criticism of tsarist institutions, he condemned any active resistance to them.

Pushkin too handled the historic situation contradictorily, but with a difference. He supported the Decembrist revolutionaries, his friends. He was a rebel writing militant early poems. Pushkin became a symbol of resistance. In the end he stood up for principle and died in a duel. He died for honor. And that difference, which is the theme of the above play, also provides the basis for our discussion of tragedy as a literary form. What is its function? Is it still viable?

Like major Russian writers who followed him, acknowledging their debt, Pushkin's name is known worldwide. But his works less; and his fame came slowly. Chinese schoolchildren read about his life and know a few poems in translation. But Westerners? The non-Russian reader cannot have the same vital enlivening response to his poetic works as to *War and Peace* and *The Brothers Karamazov*. This is because Pushkin doesn't translate.* That style like no other cannot be rendered. We only hope our own attempts, in the play, aren't quite so pitiful.

Pushkin is compared to Goethe, or the young Goethe: galvanizing lyrics; *Godunov—Götz; Yevgeny Onyegin—Werther,* the earlier *Faust;* also folktales, epigrams, satire. Pushkin is said not to 'have philosophy', that schwung of abstraction Goethe came more and more to live by. But Pushkin, like Goethe at his best, does better: his writings live ideas in a dialectical movement like reality itself. His thought made flesh goes all the way, and this is the secret of his engaging genius. Life's power, critical moments, explosive collisions are caught in a pure classical form. The sacred fire blazes yet warms; he is always struggling, learning, developing. But how often Goethe the Olympian in later years seems at a loss for subjects: to write for the sake of it, for stimulation; and then wit, nature studies, self-conscious classicism, endless aphorisms and 'orphic' wisdom, even moralizing in *Wanderjahre,* replace vital life. His magisterial relation to society and the struggles of his age was not like the persecuted Pushkin's.

We believe Pushkin's peers would be Sappho—if more remained—and Li Bai (Li Po) the Taoist-nature poet whose works are yet a great human comedy of China. These three of the world's greatest poets—along with the one true epic, *The Iliad,* and Dante's didactic epic; the Greek tragic poets, Shakespeare, and yes, *Faust*—are not translatable.

---

*The western critic said of the Russian classics: 'A handful of novelists don't make a tradsion'. But could he read Russian? Pushkin, Griboyedov, Gogol, Nekrasov, Chernyshevsky and how many others were all but a closed book to him. With the usual arrogance of the self-respecting Western intellectual, he engaged the Russian tradition no better than he did the great struggles of his era. Moreover, Russian literary tradition offers chronologic parallels to Germany's—in the writers and trends leading to and from Goethe and Pushkin. *Igor's Campaign,* Слово о пльку Игоревть, the greatest Russian literary work before Pushkin, was written c. 1185. The 18th Century writer and scientist Lomonosov might be called a Russian Lessing ... In 1775 Schweitzer's Italianate opera *Alcestis* was seen as a great step forward for German culture hitherto dependent on Italy for opera and France for drama; it was in German, sung by Germans.

But there is another thing about Pushkin: his life.
ian schoolchild learns, or did before 1991, the stor
against a Frenchman. It is part of the cultural patri
is more: an ethical cornerstone, a kind of shining e
all. Not for nothing did the great Russian revolutionary Chernyshevsky* write a small book, masterful pamphlet, about
Pushkin. For in this personal struggle was the national destiny,
it seemed, made manifest: the choice, and the way that lay
ahead. You felt it: the pathos and immediacy of tragedy which
Pushkin said was necessary to *affect the masses:* 'Drama was born
in a public square,' he had written; 'it formed a popular enter-
tainment. The people . . . require diversion, action. Drama pres-
ents them with an unusual, strange event . . . strong sensations.'
For into his story, its human terms, sensuous and direct as he
was, went the historical forces of a time and era in history: the
struggle of social classes and political trends. His drama reflects
a key turning in the social-historical development of Russia.
And we may read in his individual conflict the world historic
struggles of his country for a century and beyond.

Pushkin's story is that of a man's principle and courage. The
'honor' invoked by the poet was not more discourse, not philosophy in a neat system which concludes; and not high-flown
phrases, 'renommage'. Instead, it was principle lived and carried through to the end: as one of the key nodal moments,
among all the other conflicts and variegated shows of a society,
which light up an age; which seem pregnant with a nation's destiny; and thus may make for a stage play later on.

In the most complex and contradictory ways the sociopoliti-
cal forces of the times—whether Russia between feudalism and
socialism; whether Elizabethan England in transition between
feudalism and the storming forward of Renaissance individual-
ism; whether the age of U.S.-led imperialism with all this means
for conflict, global struggle, 'new forms of barbarism'—: the his-

---

*Tolstoy has a character in his play *Living Corpse* say Chernyshevsky's
novel *What Is to Be Done?* is boring. This novel—the most influential of all
novels inside Russia—gave 'a charge to last a lifetime' to a revolutionary
generation; it was like Rousseau, mutatis mutandis, helping prepare conditions for one of the world's great revolutions. Tolstoy (who understood
Rousseau, but not Chernyshevsky) never turned that corner; he, the great
novelist, is incomplete.

torical forces affect and form the dramatic physiognomy of the representative character. Only by living in and among the over-riding issues of an era, and at moments when the debate attains at least some intensity toward a decisive confrontation, will a dramatic character come alive in conflict however purely 'personal' it may appear.

Of course for the sake of movement and clarity a play fore-shortens real life; it combines key moments; it can present in a scene what took weeks to happen. Plot concentrates, character consolidates: in our case leaning heavily on the documented history*, like a tragedy on crutches.

Pushkin material has that advantage for the playwright: the public nature of the conflict. When Petersburg society is seen at a dress ball where the poet is all the rage pro and con, or in the street during his funeral services: this acts as a chorus. It is the essence of public life: playing a gamut of representative social attitudes and reactions to a central conflict. This chorus isn't a main character concentrated on the action like Aeschylus' Eu-menides. It is more like a leavening in the plot movement, but no less realistic and participatory, giving a sense of the historic forces at work in a character's destiny. Aeschylus makes us sense the old matriarchal society fighting to preserve itself ver-sus the emerging patriarchal relations led on by Apollo. But our modern life with its 'freer' accidental relations (seeming freer on the surface; in fact more subservient to the power of money, cap-ital) has atomized and compartmentalized social relations, un-dermining the public nature of drama embodied by the chorus in ancient society. Nowadays we have a world of trivia on TV and in the theater. Well, hopefully you'll buy something. But it seems what's truly important must be hid.

---

*Beginning with the Moscow Academy of Science's Bicentennial Pushkin Edition, Полное собрание сочинений, in 19 volumes, with every version, variant, stroke of the poet's pen. Also Shchegolev's Дуэль и смерть Пушкина deserves mention. But of all the library of writings on Pushkin we believe Lunacharsky's—more than Tomashevsky's—are the most intimate and insightful. Lunacharsky is a major critic; his Очерки по истории русской литературы is the best book ever written on Russian liter-ature. Both it and his Marxist survey of Western literature were conceived as lectures at Sverdlov University. Neither was ever translated: the West chooses to ignore the great Bolshevik writer.

Tragedy as Taboo

The tragedies of ancient Greece seem carved in the Pentelic marble of fate, and some god's whim on high Olympus. *Oedipus* may be a 'tragedy of characterization', his go-get-'em hubris predisposing; but there was still the curse on his family. The hero turned out grand, but he was a poor overbearing guy. Did he ever have a say in the facts of his life? The curse was on long before he saw the light. His consort Jocasta also learned the hard way you can't do an end run round an oracle: namely that man has a destiny for better or worse on this planet; and all the evasions and denial, miscomprehensions, trivialization, will only bring him closer to the crossroads.

It was a time of rendings. There was plague in the land, growing social antagonism. This was the stuff of tragedy: polarization, the heightening of forces toward crisis and climax. The fate of nations may be read in their great books. And the fate of Oedipus is a nation's fate centralized in a single movement: a 'unity' or totality of movement toward a tragic recognition.

Note the profound unlimited sense of life's movement, richness, aroused by this catastrophic collision. There is not only death. There is a courageous generosity and a new and shining opening up to life. Yes, in tragedy there is a glorification of human greatness, and maybe the best one. What distinguishes politician from historic figure? It is action that goes all the way; it is death, courage; it is human struggle versus the horrors of a transitional society which itself needs to die because unable to meet life's needs, and yet it cannot, and maybe for a long time. In Prometheus, in Oedipus, we feel the excitement and heightening of new possibilities—realized in concentration round a central conflict, hero, man or woman, since world history was in the lists.

We repeat: not that the tragic figure need be mythic, or a world-beater. It could be the most homely and personal of next door neighbors—a brook through your backyard, and yet a tributary somehow, however tiny, to the great ocean river of world history. The tragic figure may be a pothead or a TV freak if at last he or she manages to stand up for something symbolic and has the ability to move us, shake us up so we feel a connection to the major conflicts of our day: that significance, like a destiny, ours. Right down on the everyday ground something happens which suggests the whence and whither of aggressive wars, in our case; evokes the genocide of peoples and children so a few corporate automatons can rule; or poses the threat to planetary survival as a reality.

On stage the great issues can be expressed only if translated into 'man and deed': making us feel not discourse but the fullness of a lived world. And this can be done only in objective struggle, action, by a real collision; not subjectively like Everyman taking on Death in the old mystery plays. There is a tragic engagement; and *for us* this confrontation must be with the same forces, generally, that control the means of cultural production in the United States.

Tragedy expresses the taboo truth. Well, good luck trying to get your play produced, if you do the needed thing. I think it may make the people you have to please, the capitalist backers and major donors, a bit uncomfortable.

Tragic Moment

So for the tragic effect to occur the protagonist's passion must be somehow involved with social-historical forces also in movement toward a collision. This is the center of dramatic unity. The tragic effect cannot be produced by an isolated individual activity, destiny: in this sense we are all tragic. Rather, it is about a society, a world in the rendings of its development: the passing of an age, the movement of humanity; and now, we may say, the Pascalian wager here below on our survival as a species. When a person's activity, conflict, tragic resolution evoke the sense of history's turnings, however indirectly, however mediated by social relations: then is the moment of tragic drama.

When there can be no more compromise, and a plot is found which engages personal fate with a world historic *flaw* expressed not usually in macro-historic terms but rather in plastic, sensuous human terms, a human not necessarily national (as at times in German classical theater, *Egmont, Wallenstein*) conflict, polarization, collision, but reflecting the greater; when characters, Lear, Hamlet, take on the colorings of Shakespeare's epoch decisive for humanity, the new individual gambit and ascendant bourgeoisie, English Revolution waiting in the wings: then is the moment of tragedy for the stage.

Wherefore False Consciousness?

A-B-C . . . Here in the United States we live in an empire. No other nation in history has developed such pervasive economic and political interests and penetration worldwide. For instance: the U.S. makes seven times the foreign investment of its next competitor, Britain, thirteen times the third, Japan. The mighty corporate interests are in the business of extracting wealth and bringing it to the capitalist center. Moreover they have a global absorbent force of water in sugar; they march to the far corners and illimited interstices of the earth extracting mineral and agricultural resources, global market profits, labor power, ever amassing more capital and more. The interests of corporate and by extension bourgeois America have been and must always be conquered, and defended, in the last resort militarily. This is the situation at present. This is who we good 'ol middle-class Americans are, historically, and also—we do it but don't know it—personally. Corporate critters from cradle to grave: from the institutions and products of our parents' lives and world to the hospital we're born in food we eat clothes we wear schools we attend jobs we work at culture we're exposed to institutions medical educational cultural juridical political all the way to the funeral parlor: we are corporate fish aswim in a corporate sea, which is polluted. No free will there. Yet.

It is a situation which must be lived, but also justified so we won't have to go around feeling guilty about being gringos, guilty America, the imperialist beast.* Culturally our system and world historic position must be defined so that we whose

---

*Also: an enemy must be made of the wide terrorist world so there will be fear at home and the Big Corporate Boys can get their juicissimo Government war contracts appropriated. And the oil which is key to global dominance must be controlled.

lives, taxes, votes support such a system and let the show go blithely on *will not know* what this U.S. predatory imperialist process from which we citizens benefit and live relatively easy—I didn't say happy—might possibly mean for all the *non*-corporate folks, out there, who 'make too many babies' of course and *whose wealth we appropriate* via our trusty corporate intermediaries with their fine proprietary deeds and titles and all the legal trappings. Oh, yes; we with our political-economic-technological might, and U.S. military, have extracted fabulous resources from other people's countries and go on doing so in exchange for a false promise of (brutal dictators, our pals, keeping the restless natives in line) democracy. We sapped their resources; we recorded record profits in transactions on their foreign-dominated markets; we drew off the vital strength of their human capital for generations, subjugating their labor force, minds and bodies.

It ain't a pretty picture.

The U.N. tells us 1.4 billion people, out there, live on less than a dollar a day, and half the world's population on less than two. Starving, or close. 280 million children do not attend school: go to work long hours at starvation wages, everyday, worldwide. Each and every day 35 thousand others, not so lucky, die of malnutrition and related causes. Well, it was their wealth, livelihood, that flew like bloody tripes in the mouths of vultures flapping steel wings to America. Can it be this causes popular anger? an urge to organize, rebel? If that was your child dying of an easily curable disease, it would. Ladies at work in a sweatshop would have to work over a thousand years to earn what the corporate CEO who had them contracted makes in a single day.

Good deal! And all on the up-and-up of course: once the bloody gringo intervention has taken place from 'Panama' to the Middle East to Indonesia. And yet, would you believe it, we Yankee Doodles as the beneficiaries of those children's death have not as yet been able to establish an American paradise out of the wealth they bequeathed us. For starters there'd have to be better culture in latterday Adam's Eden than the godawful truck produced and distributed here. Take TV—please! I think I'm the only American who doesn't own one. Ten hours per day per U.S. household that thing is poisoning the mental atmosphere, emitting its false corporate consciousness—5 hours per person everyday including infants aged 0–2 who, say the few scientific studies on the subject, should never be put in front of one. TV is a drug. It bends and breaks learning curves.

But no, I'm totally wrong. Our kids, and their parents too! learn a whole lot from television. They learn manipulative trivia; corporate antisocial ideology and lies all day and night; absolutely irresponsible violence and sex; infernal self-seeking; all the pathological behavior at the heart of capital. False consciousness: to desensitize. *For the corporate forces in control of the U.S. superstructure including culture will have as little as possible to do with a vivid and vital dramatization of the major issues confronting us as a people—of which they themselves, the corporate ruling class, are the central and primary issue and contradiction.* They will use all their power to isolate and blight any new emanation of a sincere, a classic art: any promise of a true national culture that might begin to try and educate and show the way, and fortify for the decisive national and international struggles ahead. Well, they know it, with their keen ruling class instinct, the boneheaded cleverness of power, and they do it too. Not around here, they insist (which now means on the planet); 'not in our lifetime'! There shall be no great literary works brought forward to put a charge of truth into our childlike people and give them a sense of human dignity, character. Cellphones, pop music systems, video games, cheap culture—but not conscience. Profit-and-loss sheets are our conscience; quarterly earnings reports are conscience. Hefty market activity—not a great book on political economy; not the needed scientific works concerning our species', nation's, planet's real nature and destiny; not pure and uncompromising books, science, courageous plays and novels. No. Never! Our scientists, writers, artists, composers better know their place as servants to the mighty Corporate System— or else silence, death. Good night to careerism. And no nuisance dissidents around here if you please; no pariah writers, showing off! Why, the very idea. Rejection, out with you, sir. Silence. Corporate culture for the best of all possible corporate systems in the best of all possible corporate worlds, e basta. From day one, which is today, until the planet's dying day, the real situation will be hidden from the irresponsible public, distorted beyond recognition, obscured with a self-indulgent romanticism. Give 'em hit tunes and *lu-u-u-uv y'all!* coupled with obsessive consumerism; laced with tried and true All-American base opportunist patriotism; consecrated by reactionary religion. Give 'em corporate culture like a cheap fuck.

Thus the political-economic role of U.S. media and culture: to obscure, defuse, 'discredit' the truth of world historic reality. And such culture permeates every phase and aspect of American behavior and national life. Such culture dampens, prevents expression of objective social forces: key issues and figures (there shall be no key figures), key moments, the parting of the ways from conformism. The crucial conflicts and collision embodied in a play's or novel's characters must be preempted by the primrosy culture of consumerism. The perception must be that to succeed and have more abundant material life for ourselves, we must say yes to this glorious U.S. system always trying to improve itself with innocuous reforms. Yes after all to our fearless corporate leaders, yes to our corporate ruling class, yes to U.S. global dominance. Anything else is communism, terrorism; anything else 'threatens our American way of life'. So shhh! Hush up! No such thing as class conflict, social class, God forbid!

And so it's trivia; and so an antisocial, anti-human culture spread thickly with sentiment; and so the big sell. But don't look for help from your Better Business Bureau, your State Attorney General, when our benevolent 'health care' system bankrupts you with or without insurance.

Yet all this denial is only possible as long as the problems and conflicts inherent in such a national no less than personal situation are deniable; as long as they do not erupt and burst into collisions, here, there, while new social forces organize and make their way on the scene.

In such a way the poet Pushkin, with his personal problem bursting into a collision, stood at his country's and people's turning of the ways. He could be suppressed, but not the idea, the example, the choice he symbolized.

His was a particular type of collision on the way toward a choice between the old and the new.

And ours?

Changing Times Theater

As new forces—of socialism, and national liberation—accumulate and appear on the world scene and seek to impose, the corporate center is at increasing pains to keep the lid on. The attempt is to prevent significant debate, a clear and typical representation of the case with all this means for attendant attitudes, confrontations, at length the test of force.

For while the inner workings like a socioeconomic neurosis of our bourgeois life still hold sway: then such typical collisions will be more avoidable and not on the political and cultural agenda. They will be made to seem external, unnecessary, and be called extremist. The clear and courageous drive toward a clarification is defused. Tragedy is unmanned, if you will, by the orchestrated illusions of our bourgeois life eager enough to barter the human essence, individual grandeur which is the stuff of tragedy—Antigone, Oedipus, Lear, Hamlet—for profits resulting from a dozen unpublicized (or at least unexplained) corporate-sponsored holocausts like Vietnam, Palestine, Angola, Indonesia, Iraq, Iran: way over there, not tragic, of course, being a mere fabrication of Leftist rant. Another country.

Hence the thoroughgoing trivialization of American theater. The corporate backers, the major donors, exercise de facto editorial control. They see to it.

But just as the unraveling of feudal relations led to the great art of the Renaissance and to Shakespeare; just as the French Revolution led to German classical drama, Goethe and Schiller, Büchner, Kleist:—so the shocks and transformations coming on at capitalism's decline and crisis might engender a new kind of live and vital theater.

What kind?

In this historic stage the way toward human liberation and thereby survival runs through the American middle class. Only through suffering and fall, in this case Krach, is the U.S. narcotized mediocrity of denial turned into a clear conflict based on the awareness of what is humanly and historically at stake.

Tragedy is a fact of life. The cultural festivals of ancient Greece related to death: transmuted it to the people's service;

since, after all, death is in chiaroscuro relationship with life's
beauty and sacred meaning.

But in a culture of denial Death must come skulking in the
back door, so to speak, and get us on our blind side. Then like
Apollo when the Greeks ignored the oracle, Death 'comes like
the night'. But blind sides, the night, unconscious culture: such
are not the stuff of a truly national theater, a classical literature.

The sculptural heroes of great drama speak and act directly,
character to character, revealing the principle involved. Their
decision seems to contain the full, complete richness of their
world. The ocean we feel in us after seeing one of Shakespeare's
tragedies is a reflection of our species life on this earth; it is the
cultural equivalent of world history. It leads via nature to the
stars—all mediated by society. It is direct: not controlled, nor de-
flected by an institution.

But on the American stage it is the institution that speaks, or
mutes. Contemporary playgoers may laugh and cry all they
like; it is as if an outsider overheard a dialogue of outsiders.* It is
a conspiracy of sentiment. Not conflicts pitched on a level of
world history, concerning what affects us most deeply (we repeat: this may be in the most personal everyday way); not the
heightening of critical tragic themes; not the historic pathos of
tragedy;—but rather an escape, a shabby manipulative one-
night stand no matter how long the run.

On 'our' stage the space of true human growth and development, hope in the face of tragedy, a way to prevail collectively as
a people, as a species—this is usurped by trivia and conformist
'bad infinity', as filler. The facts of our life, the nation's life, are
obscured so there will be no urging of a confrontation with
them.

I'm afraid in this development our prestigious dramatists
have not helped. After all they wanted to get themselves in view
on a mainstream stage; someday have a stage named after them.
Publish, therefore, *and* perish.

But, if we know what's good for us, we'll forget such names
and look around at our society in a mess and finally get started
building a . . . theater for the changing times.

---

*Commodity—alienation; not: *for us.*

*'. . . In the really great dramatists of
the past, the tragic downfall has
always released the greatest human
energies, the supremest human heroism;
and this ennoblement of man was only
possible because the conflict was fought
out to the end.'*

If this is true, and if as we believe all 'our' American and in fact bourgeois Western theater is a thing of alienation, at its best (say in Ibsen) a passive tragedy, of omission—then what is to be done? Of course there are many attempts to express the vital life, the great issues of the day. But, looking around, what do we see in effect on our more prominent stages besides a prevalent false consciousness whose world outlook behind the scenes amounts to a style, a method tending to suppress the global conflict in progress, our struggle toward the next necessary era and period of human development?

Wherefore tragedy?

Greek tragedy might be about the Heroic Age, myths and gods, but it was also vitally topical. It addressed the key issues of the day. Those plays about individuals, colossal mythical figures, Prometheus washed about with cosmos, exhorted to principled action, and held up the banner of truth, and Man's dignity.

The historic subject matter of Shakespeare's chronicle and Roman plays, his great tragedies, had a living affinity with the vital problems of his time. For his was an art of the people, and the life of his plays grew out of the popular life past and present: the rich complex links of experience and tendency between the two.*

Pushkin in his one great full-length play, *Boris Godunov,* also shows a generalization of character and tragic destiny which

---

*I never cared about discussion of Shakespeare's 'true identity'. But listen to Lunacharsky's idea: the Earl of Rutland—who was nicknamed 'Shakespeare' in his younger years, and who fitted the bill better in some ways than an untraveled actor who misspelled a word in his will—could not have signed his name, as a matter of class consciousness, to such plays . . . Shakespeare's 'philosophy' is an aristocratic humanism.

spans the eras. The explosive scenes, in a framework of strict historic necessity, achieve a typicality seen only in Shakespeare.

This is what today's theater has lost: the vital connection with the real—not conformist: we might say commodified—life of the people: our historic struggles, our dialectical life going on like a secret known by all. And apart from this all is pretention. It could be pretention with genius à la French *tragédie classique:* art of the court divorced from the popular life, and so given over to distortions, lack of dramatic proportion; to an arbitrariness, anti-historical. And it would still be pretentiousness, in our case, with careerism.

A prerequisite of careerism is eviscerated history: acceptance of present reality divorced from a history which can only pose in its immutable 'objectivity'—for the scholars of a dominant class. This is history of the official story: no vital ties to the present, affinities, dialectics. But only through struggles with reality does our knowledge and understanding of its objects gain enrichment and precision, efficacity, for the next struggles. We see the past ever more clearly through the heightened vision attained in present struggles. The past conditioned and determined these—the present goes on determining, destining (bestimmend) the past.

Catharsis

Now with history in the works we see Pushkin's life and tragedy as a key transition. He stood on the concourse of eras as his nation's destiny began turning from serfdom toward the attempt of a world historic leap, at length, over the epoch of capitalism.

And, similarly, a tragedy of today must seem to implicate a class. This means it has to start from scratch at least for the production and distribution. Who will help it? Neither the producers of our 'major' plays—that corporate class—nor the general run of much-corrupted theatergoers has a keen taste or supposed need for such a stage.

But tragedy needs *them*—no less than Uncle Sam. And it has

them marked: our updated version of Nesselrodes, Benkendorfs, Dolgorukovs. It is pointing at all those who deny reality
and the formative working of its tragic catharsis.

Catharsis is the classical underpinning of a real, a true national culture—such as Pushkin's works initiated in Russia.

We fear it may take more than any cultural experience for the
United States of America to begin seeking and knowing itself,
like Oedipus. What sort of tragic shudder will be required to
shake us up and make us look around at the real world—at ourselves—and begin to see something? Well, the role of a real culture would be to teach, and help us turn this tragic real-life
shudder to account.

The cathartic effect is the subjective basis of the historic turning, the objective breakthrough.

We repeat and repeat: either it is a great new period, socialism
for us, or else death maybe not so slow, a tragedy with no catharsis, for the planet and our chances on it.

How then to open up space on the national stage for the real
thing, the 'real day': for the catharsis that opens eyes, and lends
the strength of a new vision—to see before it is too late?

Chekhov once said: It is good to be a writer when there is a
Tolstoy . . . who opens up space for sincere art, and consigns all
the commercial trash, the commodity art to its rightful place.

In the Corporate Age it is death, rejection at an early age, for
Tolstoy. No great writers here, if you please.

Not yet!

Will Do

For a century after his early death Pushkin's example, in the
most unforeseeable life-bestowing way, lit a path. That path of
principle, 'honor' as the nobleman called it, led through a Nine-
teenth Century flourishing in all the arts, and encouraged and
prepared revolutionary Russia. Pushkin never meant to die in a
duel nor could he foresee the immense ideological importance
of such a stance. But he did mean to play his part: do what he
could, what he said. And so he helped give his people their

chance. With his work, life, example, he assisted in the birth of a new world.

Pushkin 'lost' himself—gave himself generously, entirely—to be found by the people at the turning of the ways.

Maybe our America—if it is a nation after all, and if it is ever to become ours, for us, not for money—is the nation of all history's nations which must lose itself in order to find itself. Maybe seeds planted here by the five continents must 'die' individually, tragically, in order to have hope of living, surviving collectively.

For if no great internationalist political movement appears on the scene here in the U.S. no less than worldwide, with a leadership which sets an example by meaning what it says, doing what it says: like figures in the vital life-giving tragedies of world history, the living periods of literature and culture—then it won't matter what kind of theater we have because there won't be anyone to go see it.

That corner must be turned, as it is in tragedy: clearly, decisively, consequentially to the end.

Or else.

Next off, in the richness of our learning experience with this first attempt at a stage play, we will try to strike closer home— not carom via tsarist Russia—ever in the hope of a breakthrough, America coming to conscience, a miracle.

The people make the only miracles.

Despite the most powerfully destructive economic, political, military forces in history, which make such an experience— catharsis on our own ground toward awareness, analysis, action—seem one of supreme difficulty: yet we must seek, work, act, hope. We are not alone. And so we will.

Mantis
July 2007

Breinigsville, PA USA
31 December 2009
229949BV00001B/2/P

Become Official.

Register as an **Official NFT Member** and receive:

- access to the complete **NFT** online database
- access to PDF's of our entire guidebook series
- the ability to rate services
- event listings
- 10% discount on **NFT** books & apparel purchased on our website
- special promotions

Receive information about discounts, special promotions and access to lots of great new online content available to **Official NFT Members** only.

Register online at www.notfortourists.com for faster service.

McLean